BODY SYMBOLISM

THE FASCINATING STUDY OF MIND-BODY COMMUNICATION, WITH SUGGESTIONS TO ENHANCE OUR BODY'S HEALING ABILITY !!!

by

Richard Rybicki, M.S.W.

DISCLAIMER

This book details the author's personal experiences with and opinions about the emotional messages contained in various diseases and injuries. The author is not a physician.

The author and publisher are providing this book and its contents on an "as is" basis and make no representations of warranties of any kind with respect to this book or its contents. The author and publisher disclaim all such representations and warranties including, for example, warranties of merchantability and healthcare for a particular purpose. In addition, the author and publisher do not represent or warrant that the information accessible via this book is accurate, complete or current.

The statements made about products and services have not been evaluated by the U.S. Food and Drug Administration. They are not intended to diagnose, treat, cure or prevent any condition or disease. Please consult your own physician or healthcare specialist regarding the suggestions and recommendations made in this book.

Except as specifically stated in this book, neither the author or publisher, nor any authors, contributors or other representatives will be liable for damages arising out of or in connection with the use of this book. This is a comprehensive limitation of liability that applies to all damages of any kind, including (without limitation) compensatory; direct, indirect or consequential damages; loss of data, income or profit; loss of or damage to property and claims of third parties.

You understand that this book is not intended as a substitute for consultation with a licensed healthcare practitioner, such as your physician. Before you begin any healthcare program, or change your lifestyle in any way, you will consult your physician or other licensed healthcare practitioner to ensure that you are in good health and that the examples contained in this book will not harm you.

This book provides content related to topics physical and/or mental health issues. As such, use of this book implies your acceptance of this disclaimer.

TABLE OF CONTENTS

INTRODUCTION

The study of psychosomatic medicine began when Humans first became aware of ourselves. In ancient cultures the interplay of mind on body was a central premise of their healing arts. A great deal of that knowledge was wasted by the Western world when religion dominated and microbes were discovered. Microscopic pathogens were given full scientific credit for our disease experience and the mind was largely relegated to the back seat.

A large step forward in the West's understanding of our mind-body connection occurred in 1956 when Dr. Hans Selye published his seminal book, *The Stress Of Life*. In that book, Dr. Selye discussed his lab experiments which demonstrated that stress can have negative impacts on the body, especially the immune system, and can even lead to disease. Dr. Selye's work validated what some early physicians knew about the connection of mind and body and stimulated his contemporary researchers to focus away from the microbe-only approach to disease.

In the 1970s there was a veritable explosion of interest in the connection between mind and body. The expansions of mind that occurred in the wondrous days of the late '60s and early '70s greatly intrigued a new batch of scientific and medical researchers.

Some, such as Dr. Timothy Leary and Dr. Richard Alpert (who later became known as Ram Dass), sought to scientifically and subjectively explore perceptions of mind that were altered through psychedelic drugs. Other researchers sought to explore how our mind could physically affect our body and found ingenious ways to monitor the body's autonomic responses in controlled experiments. This was a time when aspects of Eastern cultures were introduced and embraced in the West (as when the Beatles popularized the Maharishi and the music of Ravi Shankar). As Westerners became more familiar with the holy men from India (called yogis), we were widely introduced to the beautiful practice of meditation. The

Yogis were reputed to be capable of meditatively using their minds to control their bodies in seemingly amazing ways. They were found to be able to control autonomic functions of heart rate, oxygen consumption, blood pressure, brain wave activity, pain thresholds, skin temperatures, muscle contractions, bleeding and blood clotting.

Western researchers found ingenious ways to monitor the yogis' and other subjects' autonomic responses in controlled experiments. They proved that we definitely could control our "involuntary" nervous system and have self-selected, conscious effects on our bodies' functioning. The study of psychosomatic medicine, relatively dormant until then, was blasted off the launching pad.

In the early '70s another wonderful advance in mind-body healing occurred. Dr. Carl Simonton, who worked as on oncologist, sparked an intense interest when he began using meditation in this treatment of people with cancer. By helping his patients focus their minds through creative visualization, he was able to help some of them aid their bodies' defenses to cope with cancer, sometimes to the point of consciously putting their cancer into remission.

In the 1980s we saw tremendous interest in other modalities exploring the connection of mind and body. Much was written and discussed about improving our health and avoiding disease through diet, exercise, meditation and, finally, our emotional experience. Acupuncture, iridology, homeopathy, rebirthing, radionics and channeling were more fully explored. Among those who made significant contributions were Dr. Lawrence LeShan, Dr. Gerald Jompolski, Dr. Herbert Benson, Dr. Bernie Siegel, Dr. Deepak Chopra and others too numerous to mention. These respected doctors have used their medical expertise and credentials to validate the importance of our emotional Life in determining the state of our body's health and healing. Appropriately, the '80s saw the birth of a new branch of the medical establishment designed to study the mind-body connection, called Psychoneuroimmunology. In 1992 the National Institute of Health went so far as to establish a new department devoted to the study of Alternative Medicine.

As a professional psychotherapist who has worked to help people in their emotional and physical healing, I want to share in this book some wonderful ideas I have learned about the power of the mind and beauty of the body. ***BODY SYMBOLISM*** speaks to both. I have written it from a metaphysical point of view because these ideas will be the next step in our culture's exploration and growth (metaphysics is the study of what is "behind" or "beyond" the physical). ***BODY SYMBOLISM*** breaks new ground in understanding our mind-body relationship by defining and thoroughly describing principles of "Metaphysical Psychosomatics."

I think many people will consider this book weird, even disturbing. Some will see it as heresy and others will see it as a quack scheme I have hatched to make money from desperate, ill people. Some may even see it as proof that I have demons guiding my every pen stroke. Others will grimace and say: Eeeeuuuuwwwww. Some, however, will contact the truth and depth of that truth expressed through these words and find their hearts lifted with a deeper connection to a loving Divinity and their own ability to heal.

This book takes on a big challenge. In this book I hope to help answer the crucial question of "Why me?" concerning disease and injury. "Why me?" is a common question and sometimes a very painful one. There are indeed reasons "Why us?" Not only regarding disease and injury, but everything in or not in our Lives. The primary reason is our choice, our selection.

Diseases and injuries, it turns out, are purposeful communications from our inner selves, meant to focus our attention on our belief-emotional experience.

BODY SYMBOLISM decodes the emotional meanings of each part of the body and reveals what different diseases and injuries mean emotionally. It contains valuable information for each person who has ever had, or ever will have, a body or a disease or injury.

Not understanding our body communications, we can sometimes get ourselves into intense difficulty. Those of us who are "science oriented" will tend to brush off a bout with influenza, bronchitis or injury and think it has "nothing to do with me." We will then ignore the body signals we are giving ourselves and usually proceed on the same emotional course as before. We will then tend to increase the frequency of our body communications, inwardly hoping those unpleasantries will get our attention to rectify our emotional difficulty. If we still don't outwardly get it, we may have to up the severity a bit to get our attention. Sometimes all the way to the grave; Lifetime after Lifetime - - until we choose to really face ourselves and grow.

I also have a concern for those who will not understand our body communications because we think a disease is "God's will" and we are not responsible. The truth to be aware of is that if we are not responsible, then we are not powerful either. Approaching ourselves through this filter of powerlessness, not understanding our body symbolic signals and not actively solving the problems we have created, we will probably get ourselves into deep or deeper trouble. No, we are not powerless. The greatest love God could demonstrate for us is to not give us suffering like some punishing warden, but to allow us to be powerful, self-determining and, therefore, responsible for creating our own Lives; even allowing us to choose suffering if we want.

Our ignorance is a *very, very* oppressive burden, one not be underestimated in how much turmoil and pain we are dealing with on our beautiful planet because of it. It is the lifting of ignorance that is this New Age in history and is our pathway into global, spiritual brotherhood.

Therefore, I hope as you read the chapters that follow, you will understand the ultra-sense and beauty these wondrous metaphysical ideas hold for all of us. I hope you will be pleased at how easy the metaphysical view of Life makes the actualization of the eternal moral verities. That is the most beautiful aspect of metaphysics: the high quality love, truth and justice it expresses.

If you have, have had, or will have one or more of the bodily disorders described in this book, please ask yourself if the dynamics postulated for that disorder or body part could pertain to you. If they do, then you have this book as a gentle guide as to what might be going on within you and some possibilities of what to do about it.

Finally, I would like to mention that in this book I have capitalized a few words usually not capitalized: Life, Humanity, Soul and Earth. I did this as a way of honoring the immense and beautiful realities these words represent. Also, for convenience I have used masculine pronouns to denote both females and males.

FROM THE DEPTH OF MY HEART

I HOPE YOU ENJOY

AND ARE HELPED

BY THIS BOOK.

CHAPTER ONE

PARADIGMS

Our beliefs are like sunglasses that are worn and looked through every moment of our Lives. We are so used to wearing our beliefs that we often forget we have them on, yet they color our view of the world. Unfortunately, most of us are ignorant of our deepest beliefs about ourselves and Life; and yet those ideas are the most important to clarify and, if necessary, change. It is with our core beliefs, our self-defining ideas, that we most directly create our world and our experience.

A belief system has a big job; it tries to explain Life. For about 100,000 years people have tried to answer six basic questions about being Human. I call these our "Quintessential Questions" because they are the highest queries we have about Earth Life. They are: 1) What am I? 2) Who am I? 3) What is the Earth all about? 4) Why am I here? 5) How do events happen? and 6) Why do events happen as they do?

In our attempt to understand Earth experience, a society decides certain answers to the above questions are true and makes those its core beliefs. These beliefs will define what is "real", what is "not real", what is to be considered and what is to be ignored. These important beliefs form an invisible bubble of thought *inside which* the society lives. Their cultural belief bubble defines Life and prescribes ways of dealing with Life.

Throughout time, societies have used mythology to express their beliefs about Life. Myths are imaginative stories which explain and organize what seemed to our ancestors to be a rather unpredictable, threatening and frightening world. Our myths have tried to explain the primal Human experiences of creation, birth, growth, health, illness, death and what is beyond death. Many cultures have used myths to create and justify laws, economics, holidays and treatment of selves and others. For example, some cultures have established religious myths to explain why they are supposed to fish and not hunt for a living.

Ancient people devoted a great deal of energy to figuring out just who or what started Earth in the first place. The ancients spent many Lifetimes arguing and fighting over what God(s) was, who God was, what God wanted, who would do God's work and what God had in mind for Humanity.

Up to our present time, Humanity has sifted through a variety of gods. Please realize that ideas about god are, of course, not actually god, just ideas about god, just *descriptions*; descriptions for which many people have killed and been killed.

A good term for a belief bubble with its attendant myths is "paradigm". The paradigms of Humanity range from the once popular idea that the world is being carried on the back of a giant turtle, to the one which says the sun revolves around the Earth, to even the current, improbable idea that our welfare is being protected by the research and development branch of the petrochemical industry.

Since our experience in Life is determined by what we believe, we would do well to examine the paradigms which have shaped Western civilization. Let us review the major premises and see how they answer the "Quintessential Questions" (What am I? Who am I? What is the Earth all about? Why am I here? How do events happen? and *Why* do events happen as they do?) and then examine what they say about our body and health. Western cultures have had two major paradigms that have tried to explain what Earth Life is all about and what makes us tick. These belief bubbles have shaped our thinking and emoting over the past two thousand years; they are the major idea-paths we took to create our current society, with all our strengths and problems. I refer to these two major belief bubbles as: "God As Outside Authority" (Paradigm One) and "Life As Random Event" (Paradigm Two).

PARADIGM ONE: GOD AS OUTSIDE AUTHORITY

Paradigm One is classic Judeo-Christian thought that started many centuries before Christ and became fully developed around 1,000 A.D. The core idea of classic Paradigm One (I'll write from the Roman Catholic point of view) says that one God created Earth and all Earth Life-forms. It goes on to say that God is a male who is separate from us, lives very far away and relates to us like a cranky, autocratic probation officer. Humanity's lot in Life is that we have to suffer on Earth. We are also supposed to obey church rules and try to win God's favor so we may someday be granted entry into an afterLife of safety and abundance. We are to achieve our admission to Heaven by developing the "feminine energy" components of our mind: our emotions, imagination and intuition. We are not to use the "masculine energy" portions of our mind; to not critically question and analyze ideas, especially about churches or institutions (we will examine feminine and masculine energy in more detail later). Indeed, we are commanded to follow selected leaders and books as lambs follow shepherds.

As far as our body is concerned, Paradigm One defines it rather harshly. It is said to be a temporary, tainted dwelling place, the prototype fashioned eons ago by God from a lump of clay. Our corporeal clay clump has several important characteristics: one, it was designed, created, activated and put here by God; two, it houses our immortal Soul; and three, it has the ugly habit of sabotaging our Soul's goal of winning God's forgiveness and favor.

Paradigm One says our body tries to accomplish this salvation-sabotage by liking pleasure. According to this belief bubble, there is a devil and he uses our body's capacity for pleasure to tempt us away from God into damnable sins of sensual gratification and pride. These will lead to God justifiably banishing us from Heaven. Thus, there is a ferocious war waging between our body and Soul, each pulling us this way and that. The classic version of this world view says the more we can rise above our sinful corporeal urges, the more "pure" we become in the sight of God. The most forbidden, vilified pleasure in this tradition, of course, has been the pleasure of sex. Thus, if our spirit was to be "saved", our body with its attendant, treacherous desires must be purged. This anti-body, anti-pleasure view is also held in several Eastern traditions.

Concerning disease and injury, Paradigm One says afflictions are loaded onto our bodies by God to either test our commitment to keeping his rules or to punish us for disobeying them (most likely the latter). Thus, in The Dark Ages it was considered a sin to assist people with disease conditions because to do so was to interfere with God's punishing will.

PARADIGM TWO: LIFE AS RANDOM EVENT

The arrival of scientific study was a masterpiece in the evolution of Human consciousness; the Human mind stretched and grew more than it had been allowed to do in centuries. From being over-immersed in feminine energy in Paradigm One, Western culture swung to the other side of our mental pendulum, into the development and exercise of masculine energy values and approaches. The scientific study of the planets, geology, evolution (especially the views of Charles Darwin), physics (especially the views of Isaac Newton) and the Industrial Revolution brought a new set of answers to the Quintessential Questions. These ideas formed Paradigm Two: "Life As Random Event" (well developed and in place by 1905).

The classic version of this (Darwinian-Newtonian) paradigm dismisses most of religion's primary premises. It says Life accidentally began eons ago in the sea and somehow stumbled and mutated its way up the evolutionary ladder to become you and me. This belief bubble goes on to say the Human body is a conglomerate of specialized biological functions which have been shaped and honed by eons of violent clashes with this "hostile" Earth environment. As it is with all plant and animal organisms, there is *no purpose* to Human Life, except to make desperate and often futile attempts at survival. A Human body, scientifically viewed, is a meta-composition of water, minerals and trace elements. Our biological components, especially our genes, are said to be our true nature, functioning together as a highly organized, TECHNE, electromagnetic-chemical machine.

Paradigm Two says the body is all that we are - - the six million year pinnacle of Natural Selection's incessant, violent push to flex its muscle and dominate the environment. Hardly transcendental, the Human body serves banal functions of fighting for survival, reproducing our species and housing our brain. Ultimately, it is our jelly-like brain that is responsible for our awareness and mental faculties, especially the highest Human ability of all, that of reason. Paradigm Two says reason is what separates us from animals and savages and we must therefore cling to a reason-above-all Life raft or else drown in a bottomless bog of fear, superstition and unbridled feelings. Emotion is seen to be uncivilized, regressive, weak and dangerous. This world view goes on to say there is only one chance at Life and time is running out for all of us. Therefore, we must make our Lives worthwhile by conquering something with gusto; by achieving and achieving and achieving to the heights of our rational brain's capacity so we can finally "be somebody". Yes, there is only one chance at Life and it is based on our time-limited, time-ravaged body, our corporeal machine; when it dies, we die. Period. Oblivion results.

Paradigm Two views ill conditions as a breakdown of the machine. Ill conditions, therefore, are great threats; they are reminders that our Life and all future awareness can be snuffed out at any moment. Our strongest, most heartfelt desires to live, love, learn and have fun mean nothing. Random death hits everyone. Random everything hits everyone!

Randomness is a core concept of Paradigm Two. It's an idea that is so thoroughly embraced and believed by so many, that it has become invisible to most of us. Randomness is a concept used to *explain* experience (it is not that experience

Paradigm Two goes on to say that even though Humanity has been evolving for tens of thousands of years, in the final, logical analysis, we are simply powerless monkey-elevates still at the mercy of blind, haphazard, circumstantial forces. If we have a mind at all, it is only because of the complexity of our brain functions. We tell ourselves stories about meaning in Life and Human virtues to fool ourselves out of the terror of being so insignificant. Death is the universe's primary, unavoidable force that haunts us all (the IRS is a close second). Unfortunately for us, this imperfect body machine that we are wears down; this is caused by getting old and lethal, parasitic agents in our violent environment, called "germs". Like tiny Red Barons, they flit about, poised ready to attack us dead. It is just a matter of chance whether we get struck down or not. We have no say in it. There is no comprehension to this random, haphazard Earth Life, filled with its multitude of perils. There is no God and there is no ordering principle; we just have to take what comes our way and cope with it. We have no influence; we either get good luck or bad luck. Too bad.

RECENT DEVELOPMENTS

Fortunately, throughout history groups of people have held views of the body and health that are neither Paradigm One nor Paradigm Two oriented. These alternative views started in the more feminine energy, Eastern cultures; from the Babylonians to the Egyptians, to the Hindu, to the Chinese and Japanese, to the Greeks, to the Island Peoples and our Native Americans. This old, amalgamated world view says people have both a mind and a body and that our mind operates as a partner with our body, as part of an interactive whole that is us. Contrary to Western paradigms, this view states that ill conditions result from a disturbance in our emotional relationship with our personal truth. This view of mind-body holism has been slowly creeping into Western medical practice. This re-thinking on the part of our medical establishment has been greatly encouraged by recent developments in the fields of hypnotism, mental training, biofeedback, parapsychology, prayer and the placebo effect (which is, actually, self-hypnosis). Added to these are the wonderful contributions being made by Chinese medicine, Ayurveda, acupuncture, herbs, acupressure, dance therapy, massage therapy, radionics, homeopathy, aroma therapy, nutrition, yoga and plain ol' laughing.

Many people did not wait for the medical establishment to sanction their beneficial treatments, as reflected in a widely quoted study in The New England Journal Of Medicine that estimates 33% of Americans spend $14 billion each year on alternative medical treatments.[1] This populous support for non-traditional means of healing led the prestigious National Institute Of Health to open an Office Of Alternative Medicine in 1992.

The prime factor in this growing shift toward a more holistic, psychosomatic view of mind-body health is the increasingly successful results being achieved by ordinary people who learn to use their thought and imagination to activate and direct their healing process. There are hundreds of centers in the world now (many more to come) which apply techniques of mental training to improving health conditions. A small version of what is yet to occur, but we are finally becoming acquainted with the tremendous power and freedom which are inherently ours and are finding out that the key to all techniques of healing and healthy living is responsibility. Yes, it seems that the chief issue for our growth and happiness now becomes whether we care enough about ourselves and whether we desire happiness enough to learn how to responsibly awaken, exercise and focus our mental abilities to build our mental and physical health.

BREAKTHROUGHS

There have been at least two recent advances in understanding the nature of Life on Earth that I think hold special significance for all people and for our future.

The first great advance has taken place through our scientific investigations into the nature of matter. This new field of scientific study is called quantum-relativistic physics. We won't discuss these theories in detail here, except to state their central discovery: modern physics realizes that the atoms which make up the objects in our world, including our bodies, are actually bits of whirring energy. These bits of energy that make up matter form electromagnetic fields that actually interact with the energy fields we call thought. The science of quantum-relativistic physics indicates that, on sub-atomic levels, each person is a small piece of a connected, tremendously interactive "web of energy" that makes up our universe. This is the Unified Field Theory in physics; it was first postulated in 1714, given modern form by Albert Einstein, given mathematical form by John Bell, applied to our brain processes by Karl Pribram and recently verified by physicist David Bohm. This unified web of energy means each person is connected to and is influencing the world around us in a subtle and intimate fashion with our thought. These ideas repudiate the mechanistic view of Isaac Newton, et al, that we are merely isolated specs in a haphazard universe with no influence on what happens to or around us.

In a wonderful, seminal book, *"The Holographic Paradigm"*, an article was included from *"The Brain/Mind Bulletin"* to explain physicist David Bohm's theory. It said in part:

> "As we will see, Bohm's work in subatomic physics and the "Quantum Potential" had led him to the conclusion that physical entities which seemed to be separate and discrete in space and time were actually linked or unified in an implicit or underlying fashion. In Bohm's terminology, under the explicate realm of

separate things and events is an implicate realm of undivided wholeness, and this implicate whole is simultaneously available to each explicate part. In other words, the physical universe itself seemed to be a gigantic hologram, with each part being in the whole and the whole being in each part.

It was at this point that "the holographic paradigm" was born: the brain is a hologram perceiving and participating in a holographic universe. In the explicate or manifest realm of space and time, things and events are indeed separate and discrete. But beneath the surface, as it were, in the implicate or frequency realm, all things and events are spacelessly, timelessly, intrinsically one and undivided."[2]

Karl Pribram, who works as a neurosurgeon and brain investigator, has added his research to David Bohm's and has strengthened the holographic paradigm. While David Bohm explored the holographic nature of reality, Karl Pribram researched the holographic mechanisms of the brain. Their theories support each other and other scientists have agreed on the possibilities:

"Parapsychologists Stanley Krippner, Charles Tart and Douglas Dean commented that the holographic model is consistent with their experimental data, particularly as it postulates access to a domain transcending time and space..."[3]

The development of the holographic paradigm is a monumental breakthrough from science in understanding the deeper nature of Earth Life. Most interestingly and reassuringly, it concurs with the information given to us by mystics throughout the centuries about the "universality (interconnectedness) of all things". Here is how the development of the holographic model has occurred:

"CHRONOLOGY OF AN IDEA"

1714- -   *Gotfried Wilhelm von Leibniz, discoverer of integral and differential calculus, said that a metaphysical reality underlies and generates the material universe. Space-time, mass and motion of physics and transfer of energies are intellectual constructs.*

1902- - *William James proposed that the brain normally filters out a larger reality.*

1905- - *Albert Einstein published his theories.*

1907- - *Henri Bergson said that the ultimate reality is a vital impulse comprehensible only by intuition. The brain screens out the larger reality.*

1929- - *Alfred Whitehead, mathematician and philosopher, described nature as a great expanding nexus of occurrences not terminating in sense perception. Dualism such as mind/matter are false; reality is inclusive and interlocking and Karl Lashley published his great body of research demonstrating that specific memory is not to be found in any particular site in the brain, but is distributed throughout.*

1947- - *Dennis Gabor employed Leibniz's calculus to describe a potential three-dimensional photography: holography.*

1965- - *Emmett Leith and Juris Upatnicks announced their successful construction of holograms with the newly invented laser beam.*

1969- - *Karl Pribram, who had worked with Lashley as a neuro-surgeon, proposed that the hologram was a powerful model for brain processes.*

1971- - *Physicist David Bohm, who had worked with Einstein, proposed that the organization of the universe may be holographic.*

1975- -   *Pribram synthesized his theories and*
         Bohm's in a German publication on
         Gestalt psychology.

1977- -   *Pribram speculated on the unifying*
         metaphysical implications of the
         synthesis. "[4]

Thus, the holographic paradigm is the latest offering from hard science to explain the underlying structure and mechanics of Earth Life. These ideas then lead to a new questions, such as: how did such an intelligent system like a holographic universe originate? And who or what did that?

The second recent breakthrough in understanding the nature of Life on Earth has occurred in a more unorthodox, but no less valid fashion. This breakthrough involves the expanded use of mental abilities, in the range we call psychic functioning. Just as there are outer senses, so are there inner senses (precognition, telepathy, etc.). Many people throughout history have demonstrated the use of their inner senses in profound ways. This has occurred more often in the Eastern cultures because of their stronger devotion to the feminine energy side of Human nature. Western cultures, though, have had a few well known demonstrators of the psychic arts, such as Edgar Cayce, Madam Blavatski and Jesus. In fact, Western civilization's bibles are replete with examples of psychic functioning, from precognitive dreams to healings, to transformations of matter. Psychic abilities, we are beginning to understand, are Human abilities, just a bit further out on the continuum of Human sensing.

One very special psychic ability is that of acting as a medium. A genuine medium can deliberately shut down his Conscious Mind and go into a trance or even travel to another realm. While away, the medium's "empty" Conscious Mind can be used to receive ideas from other realms, just as one can hear a message on an open CB frequency.

One medium I have heard a lot about and who died a while ago is named Jane Roberts. Ms. Roberts had the amazing psychic ability to go into a trance and allow a non-physical entity called Seth to speak through her body; it was sort of a psychic-lease program. Ms. Roberts would go into a trance and Seth would come through and dictate profound discourses on the nature of Earth Life and the inner workings of Humanity. This information was printed and is available from Prentice-Hall Publishing. I have read many of Seth's works and encourage everyone who wants to learn more about metaphysics to read these illuminating and inspiring books. They were most helpful to me in my awakening. I passionately wanted to meet Jane Roberts and Seth; unfortunately, a meeting was impossible to arrange. Though I understood their reasons, I felt disappointed because I wanted to research the channeling phenomenon for myself, especially since the information was so wonderful and I did not want it to be a scam.

In 1975 I was teaching a course about using more of our mental abilities. We learned how to consciously lower our brain waves to improve learning, improve memory, reduce pain and enhance creativity. Most important to me, I actually taught people how to use their psychic abilities! Everyone who took my class reported to have had a psychic experience. The name of that class is Silva Mind Control and I had a huge amount of fun teaching it.

Through one of my students, I learned that one of his good friends had recently opened up the ability to act as a channel for a non-physical entity. I eagerly and quickly signed up for a reading; finally, this was my chance to investigate! I met the channeling person and the non-physical entity who speaks through him on July 25, 1975. I skeptically and seriously investigated this phenomenon for myself by having consultations with the entity over the course of several years, having over a hundred readings. I asked questions about my Life that were very personal and involved. Over time, I proved to my skeptical self that this channeling phenomenon was real and that I had indeed been fortunate to meet an entity who has an awareness that is way beyond that of Humanity's.

Though this may seem incredulous and even absurd to some of you, I assure you it is true. I have personally investigated the phenomenon since 1975 and I continue to be amazed and helped by the beauty, wisdom, love and humor of the entity's messages. The Human who channels the entity is named Jach and the entity is called Lazaris.

Lazaris says he has never had a physical Lifetime and that he resides in a dimension that is very different from ours. Because he lives outside our Earthly set, he can offer us insights that we can dearly use, especially facing the problems of our world now.

Lazaris, though an expanded being, is not communicating with us to save Humanity or to start a cult. He is sharing ideas that are loving and helpful and we are invited to explore them and, if we like those ideas, use them to better create our preferred future. I was very skeptical when I started to investigate Lazaris and his ideas and I wholeheartedly encourage everyone to approach similarly. But please do yourselves the favor of exploring the uplifting and very helpful ideas Lazaris has to share. I know my Life has been enriched to a tremendous degree because of the profound help I have received through knowing Lazaris.

The second great advance in understanding the nature of Life on Earth has come from these and other non-physical guests. Their expansive ideas are greatly enhancing and accelerating our investigations into the deeper nature of Earth Life.

PHILOSOPHIC GROWTH

Like concentric rings which radiate outwardly when a pebble is dropped into water, the Human race moves forth in its development, ever expanding beyond previous mental territory. The waves of Human expansion of the past (which include language, fire, the wheel, alphabets, the printing press, electromagnetics, microbes, flight, etc.) have carried Humanity to the point of evolution in which we are now faced with our grandest challenge yet: to develop in the most meaningful way we can, to move beyond survival and into our spirituality. Thus, our evolutionary focus is to become more lovingly involved with all forms of Life. This is the significance of the trend toward holistic medicine, to demonstrate the power of our minds to lovingly realign our bodies into harmony and remove ill and/or injured conditions. We also see that as we lovingly take charge of our minds and bodies we can branch out to similarly influence other levels of our environment; our families and friends, plants and animals, neighborhoods, weather, cities, regions, country, countries, world village and even the Earth herself.

What we culturally yearn for is the crest of the next wave of philosophic revolution on which we can surf into the evolutionary thrill of spiritual adulthood. I believe that grand philosophic growth is now here; it is the beautiful study of metaphysics, which is the philosophic basis for this study of Body Symbolism.

PARADIGM THREE: THE METAPHYSICAL VIEW OF EARTH LIFE

To facilitate our discussion of Body Symbolism, for those of you who are not yet familiar with metaphysics, we will now consider an overview of *the next wave of world philosophic revolution,* Paradigm Three, the metaphysical view of Life on Earth. This presentation is an amalgam of ideas I have learned from several sources, Human and non-Human. Some of these ideas are well known and others are not. I encourage you to seriously consider them as they *will* have a large impact on our future.

It is interesting how we Humans discover more and more about our world. In 200 B.C., for instance, people knew nothing about electromagnetism, yet it was here, surrounding us all the time.

Eventually we "bumped" into it, understood it and harnessed it, so now we barely even think about the mechanics involved with we turn on our radios, TVs or computers. In the same way, metaphysics and Body Symbolism have *always* been operative, we just have not known it. We are just now understanding these deepest dynamics of Earth Life, even though we have been operating in the Earth system for many thousands of years!

Though succinct, the discussion which follows will likely be enjoyable because these are beautiful, affirming ideas about Life. In brief, Paradigm Three, metaphysics, states:

1) Every Earth thing, event and every bit of Life (i.e. consciousness) is made up of energy that is alive, aware and, in its own way, consciously evolving. The root energy of every being, every thing and every event is love. There is *no* spot where there is no love. One Source started all of Life off by pondering itself; love is the root identity and curiosity and thought are the root actions. Each bit of Life is a unique manifestation of The Source's primal drive to explore its inner nature and actualize its inherent excellence through free will. There are many, many different species of consciousness living in billions of different dimensions and worlds.

Each dimension can be likened to an aquarium; sometimes there is contact between beings in different aquariums (as when Seth, Lazaris or "angels" communicate with us). All of Life is good, powerful and imbued with beauty, even under a mask of seeming cruelty. Love and joy are ever-present possibilities available to any consciousness, as it prefers.

2)   The basic law operative throughout the billions of different worlds may be called "The Great Principle Of Reflectivity". It is a beautiful and glorious principle through which every entity operates as it seeks its evolutionary, mental-emotional fulfillment. Because our basic nature is that of living awareness (consciousness), the basic law of all realities is: mind uses the "primal" Life energies of thought, emotion and imagination to shape and maintain the "secondary" energies of event and matter. The Great Principle Of Reflectivity operates to make each dimension, each universe and each individual Life a living feedback system. This means our mental experience is scientifically, "magically", metaphysically projected outward and then experienced as our day-to-day, personal reality. *Each individual, moment to moment,*

determines the objects and events in or not in his Life by the type and quality of his conscious and unconscious thought, emotion and imagination.

When we are physical, our bodies are like a hologram living inside a holographic world. Everything physical is made up of the same material: whirring light energy. When we are inside our physical holographic world, it seems solid to us and has dimension. We can say that each of us lives in and creates the conditions inside our own, personal Life-sphere, a "Thought Created, Thought Controlled Holographic Bubble" (TCTCHB).

What this means is that with the deep portions of our Inner Selves, we create an energy bubble in which our outer self, us, lives. Inside this seemingly solid and infinite Life bubble we have various experiences, both happy and unhappy. We are like playwrights who write a play and create a magical stage on which holographic props appear as needed, as thought up. We playwrights then become the lead characters in our own play and act out the emotional and moral lessons to be learned. The props and experiences in or not in our play are symbolic of our psychological states. Everything physical is feedback of where we are in our mental and emotional development. All scripts and mind sets are open to re-selection at any time. No one is trapped within their play unwillingly.

According to metaphysics, every bit of experience we have occurs inside our TCTCHB, our personal Life-sphere, and is consciously or unconsciously selected by us; nothing is random and there are no accidents. Lazaris says every Human uses the same mental raw materials and tools to create our reality. Our six raw materials are: our beliefs and attitudes, our thoughts and feelings and our choices and decisions. The three mental tools we use are: our desire, imagination and expectation. As we mix and match these nine elements on our mental baking pan, so results the type of cookies we will produce. Negative beliefs and negative thoughts always make for distasteful realities. It is most important to know that all thoughts are experience requisitions. According to Paradigm Three, we are, moment to moment, choosing our experience and, moment to moment, translating our Lives into this sentence: *"Look what I am giving myself now."* Physical reality gives back exactly what was offered; it is set up to be pure, symbolic feedback. This means that if I go to start my car in the morning and find out that my battery is dead, I have to ask myself why did I allow this to happen? What does this mean to me? Most of us now would think this has nothing to do with me, that the battery just expired and it happened to (randomly) happen today. Nope, not so. The living feedback system of Earth reality is designed to help you and I, budding creators that we are, understand and evaluate the contents of our beliefs and emotions. We want to do this so we can consciously change our minds away from the unloving and painful and grow toward the most loving. This is called maturity; it produces the most fun. It is very important to understand that nothing can counter our conscious free will except our unconscious free will.

I would like to quote a section from my second book, *The Importance Of Being Human*,[5] to illustrate our moment to moment interaction with the Great Principle Of Reflectivity:

"FRANCOIS

....Let us suppose we have a small garden and hire a French fellow to tend the garden and his name is Francois. Let us also assume that we have six very, very special electroquasaro-plasma-magneto generators and we secretly place them surrounding the garden and camouflage them very well. Let us also say that these rare electroquasaro-plasma-magneto generators are creating a very special electromagnetic field, so that when a person thinks a thought of sufficient intensity, the thought energy emitted hits the super, ultra-charged field and POOF! the thought energy is greatly amplified and immediately turns into the object or event thought about. Some generators, eh? Wouldn't you just love to have some?

Enter Francois, turn on the generators, settle back and watch the show. First thing, Francois greets the garden and the flowers. He bows to them and wishes for their health. He pledges himself to work toward their happiness using all his horticultural knowledge and abilities, with love. POOF! All plants in the garden immediately grow two inches. He then walks to the tool shed and remembers that he left his new tape measurer at home and wishes like heck he had it with him and POOF! He suddenly sees his tape measurer laying at this feet. Francois becomes delighted that he did not forget it after all and prides himself on having a rather good memory. POOF! Francois experiences a strengthening of memory functions and many previously forgotten details of his Life suddenly go whizzing through his awareness, causing him to feel rather dazed and spaced out. Francois takes his tape measurer, his strengthened memory and a few other tools and staggers over to a new patch of crabgrass, props himself up and thinks: 'Crabgrass? Again? Oi vey! Crabgrass! Poor Francois, he tries and tries, but just can't win against crabgrass! It's too tough, too...tooo...' ZAP!!! ZAP!!! ZAP!!! Suddenly, there's Francois, standing in a patch of wildly growing, ravaging crabgrass that's five feet high already! He shakes his bug-eyed head in great disbelief and fear: 'Hey, wazza madder???? Hey, dat can't happen!' POOF! The crabgrass shrinks to its previous level. Right about now, the perplexed, panting Francois either thinks this is one screwy garden or he's going nuts!! For his sake, I hope he thinks the first thought...."

Well, that's it, folks. That's what has been going on with us throughout history and that's what is going on with us right now: that's it! Taaa-daa! The nature of physical reality is such that it centers around what I call The Great Principle Of Reflectivity. Taaa-daaa! That is, our world, like Francois' garden, is a reflective experience, a living feedback system. Our world is bathed in a living energy which is programmed to interact with thought. Our inner desires are transformed into objects and events as surely as a tadpole is transformed into a frog.

Simple, isn't it? And what poetic justice to it, too! If Francois thinks of apples, he'll create apples. If he thinks of goblins, he'll create goblins. In whichever direction Francois takes his thought, that will become manifest, will become his temporary camouflage reality until he changes that thought to create a new reality. And when I sat create, I mean *create!* No one thrusts upon Francois any of the experiences he had in the garden.   His environment had a basically passive nature to it with Francois being the active one, *the thought emitting one.*

3) The Earth learning system was established eons ago. Each person who is here now is here because of an inner decision to be here; we come to Earth - - many times, many incarnations - - for lessons in how to love and think well.

We have thousands of physical Lifetimes to give ourselves maximum exposure to the Earth system. We do this because learning on Earth is more emotionally intense and therefore quicker than it is in other dimensions. The intensity of Earth Life makes it an attractive, quick-paced place to get the hang of consciously creating realities.

So, what is Earth? A school; a feedback school we are creating and living in. Earth is an institution of higher learning; learning about self, conscious evolution and fun. All of us have chosen to attend; we have come here to learn how to create well, to learn how to think well. We have come to Earth (again) to consciously change. We've come here to grow up. We have come here to grow up in responsibility, creativity and love (the most fun). We are here to discover our power to imagine the experiences we desire and to give them to ourselves, inside our own "Thought Created, Thought Controlled Holographic Bubble". We have come here, to Earth, to beautiful Earth, to discover who we really are: Creators! Sparks of imagination, power, beauty and love. Ultimately, after however many Lifetimes we may need, all Human consciousness will choose non-violence and love.

Most importantly, we have come to Earth again to grow in our spirituality. Many of us have been taught spirituality is only Paradigm One oriented; dreary, dull and sometimes painful. Actually, not so. The New Spirituality is a truer vision of this most important aspect of our Human nature. Our spirituality is our personal relationship to the Source Of All, the Divinity, Goddess-God (I refer to The Divinity as Goddess-God to acknowledge the feminine energy-masculine energy nature of The Source). Our spirituality is us feeding and nurturing the part of us that wants so desperately to love ourselves, our Lives and, by logical and emotional extension, The Source Of All Life. Our spirituality also involves a relationship with the piece of The Source who directly created us and all our physical Lifetimes, our Higher Self.

A most important point: as we understand the wonderful gift Goddess-God has given us - - to be able to choose our own experience - - then we see that the supreme value of justice is thoroughly woven into the very structure of physical reality. Our experiences are not occurring randomly and no one is forcing us to have the experiences we have. We can extrapolate from this glorious gift of justice, because it allows us the most freedom, that love and success are the underlying values of the cosmos and Goddess-God. Now we have more reason to open our hearts, reconnect and invite Goddess-God back into our Lives and societies. This is the basis of The New Spirituality.

4) All people are inherently good, incredibly powerful and able to live in a state of self-harmony, abundance, health and fun once we learn how to give these gifts to ourselves, once we learn how to love. Some loving people, however, will not select these gifts this Lifetime because we have other plans for achieving our growth.

5) We live in several environments at once, like concentric circles they radiate: there's imagination, thought, emotion, aura, body, family, neighborhood, society, air, Earth, solar system, galaxy and so on. In a micro-macro fashion we are metaphysically connected to and create each sphere of activity with our individual thoughts. Our thoughts and emotions, for example, determine our weather.

6) As we would put on and wear a scuba suit to operate under water, so we must create and wear a body-suit to operate in our physical world. Moment to moment our Inner Self creates our holographic body beneath our awareness (just as moment to moment our heart pumps blood and our fingernails grow, all

beneath our conscious awareness). Operating in harmony with The Great Principle Of Reflectivity, the physical aspects of our body (its health, vitality, color, posture, proportions, movements, tensions, etc.) reflect the current mental-emotional state of the being who resides within. There is, in its deepest essence, nothing physical about our body - - it is a total creation and *representation* of our conscious and unconscious thought and emotion. We are free to change its conditions as we desire. We are also free to die, when and how we desire.

Our challenge and opportunity is to evaluate these ideas for ourselves and make a choice for our growth, to experiment with them or not. It is my sincere conviction, on several levels of my being, that these principles do indeed operate as the structure of our beloved Earth aquarium and beyond.

Thousands of people have known about and have read Seth's and Jane Roberts' books and hundreds of thousands of people know about and have explored my dear, non-physical friend, Lazaris. They have met with Lazaris in large groups, had personal consultations and have listened to taped lectures. These thousands of people, plus thousands who are studying metaphysical ideas from other sources (Human or not), are slowly changing their beliefs about Earth Life and themselves and embracing the metaphysical view. They are taking the risk of leaving the cozy nest of Paradigm One - Paradigm Two ideas to venture forth and go for the rewards available through expanded thought and an expanding self.

OUR BODY

The focus of this book is our beloved body. We will view the impacts of mind on body mentioned earlier - - hypnotism, placebo effect, remission - - through a metaphysical perspective. Mind, according to metaphysics, not only influences the body directly, it creates the body directly. Moment to moment.

A Human body is a pal. Our body is a gift from us to us; it is our cozy holographic home away from home. But more than that, our body is what our Unconscious Mind is doing as our Unconscious Mind intersects with this Lifetime's energy field. Our body is Life, pure and holy.

Our Inner Self programs energy into invisible light and inaudible sound, weaving these into electromagnetic patterns which coalesce into the cells, tissues, organs and organ systems we are now *wearing*. These components of our body have an over-all biological consciousness which is dedicated to survival, their main hobby. The energy we use to form our body is the same energy used to think, grow nectarines and heal wounds. This sharing of Life energy is the primary connection amongst all consciousness and their forms; one battery, many illusions.

It follows from The Great Principle Of Reflectivity that our body, like all else in our illusionary, Thought Created, Thought Controlled Holographic Bubble, reflects our spiritual-psychological states to us. Our body is a living symbol, a bio-representation of our current thought and emotion.

I imagine some of the ideas recently stated are difficult for many of us to accept. Especially the last sentence in the above paragraph. I am sure some of us are incredulous about the idea that we create all our bodily disturbances with our mind. Some people think Humans cannot create anything without God's direct involvement. Others think Paradigm Two is the way to go: what about the physical factors, they ask? What about bacteria? What about toxic wastes? What about viruses? What about obesity? What about pesticides? What about genetics? What about high fat diets? What about Bovine Growth Hormone? What about slippery floors or unsafe cars? What about hurtful people?

Yes, of course these are viable factors in disease and injury constructions. I do not discount their negative impacts, nor do I encourage people to ignore them and "just think positively". The physical factors listed above, plus poor nutrition, sound pollution, ultra-violet rays, odor pollution (cigarettes), visual ugliness (especially litter and graffiti) and even bumpy roads can have negative impacts on our health and well-being. No doubt about it. As it turns out, however, Humans are much more complex than dealing with just the physical factors.

Whenever we analyze reasons for creating our experience, we would do well to inspect them on two levels at the same time: micro and macro. The micro level of Human affairs is the level in which we are focused most of the time and are most accustomed to: our day-to-day reality. The micro level involves how our Child Within feels about the impacts daily events have upon us. It also includes the impacts we have on others and the impacts our hour-to-hour thoughts, feelings, imaginings and expectations have on us.

The macro level is very different; it is the metaphysical realm - - the level of which most of us are most often unaware. On the macro level we go to the bank; we invest our psychic energy in possible realities by consciously and unconsciously focusing on them. When we think a certain way, when we build up certain feelings and when we engage in certain fantasies, we are investing our psychic energy in those experiences. When enough mental and emotional energy is invested in certain possible realities, we attract them to us. It is as if they become "heavy enough" with the energy of our intent and they "drop", so to speak, "down" to us into our holographic world and we encounter them as our daily events (re: "Look what I am giving myself now!"). It is on the macro level, for instance, that we decide we want a bout with bronchitis to symbolize our clogged-up sadness. Also, it is on the macro level that our Soul and Higher Self may arrange negative experiences to signal us that we are on the wrong track.

On the micro level, we may be chewing tobacco and spittin'
on the sidewalk, thinking that smokeless tobacco may cause cancer,
but so what? It is on the macro level that we choose the condition
of cancer and purposely place it in our mouth to signal blocked
expression of raging anger.

Here is another example of how we work: on the day-to-
day, micro level we may be over-exposed to radiation from nuclear
explosions in which our government cruelly uses us as guinea pigs
to test Human tolerance (this actually happened). On the macro
level, we choose cancer of the blood to signal feeling angrily
betrayed by our family, even the "family" of our country
(government). Or, on the micro level, we may experience
stillbirths, cancers and genetic mutations because of toxic wastes
buried beneath our housing developments. On the macro level, we
congregate to possibly symbolize victimhood, raging angers and
desires for community.

Many people engaged in alternative healing are focusing on
restoring balance inside the body. This is a wonderful contribution
that can be immensely beneficial. They, however, are addressing
symptoms on the physical, micro level, rather than the causes on the

macro, emotional level. This even pertains to genetics. More than ever, genes are being put into the societal spotlight as the causation of disease; from diabetes to heart problems, to breast cancer, etc. Our researchers are creating wonderful information about the mechanisms of the Human body. Manipulating the physical process of our body may indeed alter the course of disease in the micro, as when bone marrow transplants are performed. This is a wonderful advance I wholeheartedly support (I know I would avail myself of those treatments if I needed to). These micro-mechanical-manipulations, however, do not alter our motives in the macro for creating the bodily problems. Thus, having not understood our macro-motives for selecting a disturbance in the first place, we may then create another, more intense disturbance to get our attention in the second place. Or, we may not; depends on our subjective, emotional experience. But it is likely.

To be most thorough in health care, our macro-motives would ideally be analyzed and understood. Unfortunately, many of us use micro dynamics as an excuse to deny our emotional communications. Sounds like: "I got sick and vomited a lot because of food poisoning, not because I repressed a lot of anger, sadness or fear at recent events about which I have turned my stomach."

Analyzing our diseases and injuries on both levels, micro and macro, is the most thorough, most effective approach. As we read on, though rather "weird" for many of us, please approach the explanations offered skeptically and openly. I think they are very beautiful and most compelling, truly worth our consideration.

To continue about the metaphysical-macro dynamics of our body: the cells we create to manifest our body are the most intimate physical allies we have. They are only too happy to do our bidding, as we direct them. Our cells will heal themselves or destroy themselves for us, as we prefer. They agree to not have free will, so they await our every mental signal. This is a wonderful clarification metaphysics offers about our body: each body state is a probability, each is mentally-emotionally induced. Nothing in Earth Life is accidental, especially in regard to our bodies. Therefore, each body state is deliberately selected to communicate a specific message; this is called Body Symbolism. Each health problem is an outer manifestation of an inner event, most often turmoil. Any disorder or symptom can have one or more emotional reasons behind it.

Remember our discussion of masculine and feminine energies which comprise a Human, even Goddess-God? Well, this is symbolized in our bodies by the right side and left side. Our right side is masculine; events occurring on the right side of our body involve either the expression of our masculine energy or issues between us and a male. Events occurring on the left side of our body involve either the expression of our feminine energy or issues between us and a female.

Great strengths and abilities are inherent in our body, waiting to be triggered by our belief, desire and action. Our mind-body alliance and, therefore, our healing abilities, can be strengthened with awareness, kindness, meditation, exercise, changing sleep patterns, honoring and programming dreams, increasing pleasure and a great deal of love.

Speaking of awareness and love, I would like to mention another non-physical being I have met who has helped me greatly. On the lovely day of May 10, 1995 I met a wonderful entity called

Galexis who is channeled by a woman named Ginger. Fortunately
for me, I have had regular sessions with them since that time and
have been helped into a much deeper understanding and
appreciation of myself and metaphysics. I know my Life has been
profoundly enhanced through the great gifts they have given me and
I am most grateful.

HEALTH

Health is a state of bodily grace. It is a condition and, like
all conditions, it is a probable condition. Who gets health? Anyone
who wants health. But why do some people have illness then?
After all, "Nobody wants to be sick." Well, since all of us live
inside our private TCTCHBs, all conditions which exist are
conditions we have attracted, for one reason or another, often
unconsciously. The Great Principle Of Reflectivity makes no
mistakes, but people sure do. And sometimes we make the serious
mistake of treating ourselves poorly. We may reflect this to
ourselves through the physical experiences called illness or injury.

As stated earlier, the cells which make up our body are our
dearest pets. Our body is not a stupid lump of reflex conditioned

clay, but an aware, buzzing colony of billions and billions of tiny aware beings who have joyously consented to serve as our body, according to the mental blueprints we think for ourselves. Our cells will serve us to the utmost; if we choose to give ourselves a disease condition, they will gladly act out that role for us. Our cells will stop working for us, will multiply crazily for us, will jerk and shriek with pain for us, will dehydrate for us, will blow themselves up for us - - whatever we'd like. The choice is ours.

Our cells care about us a great deal and are so wonderfully loyal, even to the point of their own physical destruction. All this they will experience for us so we can get our own attention and finally confront our psychological issues. Symptomized cells are urging us to remove whatever self-limiting emotional patterns we and they are living out.

All diseases and all symptoms have meaning; nothing is accidental. Body Symbolism operates through each part of our body.

For one reason or another we choose our unpleasant experiences. It is highly recommended that we not get down on ourselves or our body for having disease conditions and symptoms. I know this is often difficult, but we always do ourselves great disservice to punish ourselves for attracting negative experiences. Of course, most of us do not enjoy rotten experiences, but if we do create them, then it is best to release our anger and then work and figure out why we have them. We must evaluate our symptoms to understand our motives. Then we can use our minds to change these motives and release the negative condition we originally attracted with our minds. However, if we blame ourselves and/or our body, we will only generate more negative vibes with which we will injure ourselves further. Plus, we will confuse ourselves as to our motives for creating the negative condition in the first place. So, as arduous as it may seem, the first step in dealing with ill conditions is to accept the experience and take responsibility for it without blaming ourselves.

A special note here: a common criticism of encouraging people to take responsibility for creating a disease or injury is that this somehow makes people feel guilty for getting sick. This is totally false and indeed a harmful approach. Taking responsibility for creating a disease or injury does not, but itself, create guilt. It actually creates freedom because we can be empowered to discover and change our motivations so as to never have to have such an experience again. If we find we are responsible for having a certain condition and we feel guilty because of it, that guilt is something we have attached to the responsibility, all on our own. It is as if someone gives us a powerful locomotive to achieve some wonderful work and we attach to it a tanker car filled with dangerous, stinking toxic waste. Then we get mad at the locomotive or the one who gave us the locomotive? The attachment of guilt to responsibility is not at all necessary. Common, yes, but not necessary. I suggest we be wary of those who want to protect us from ourselves by telling us we are not responsible for our own creations. If we feel guilty about our unpleasant events (which I can well understand), then it is our job to work it through and release the guilt, primarily by expressing anger at ourselves (without harm) and then forgiving ourselves. Please remember, responsibility in no way brings self-blame or guilt. Actually, Responsibility = Power = Options = Freedom. We can measure our psychological progress as our feedback symptoms subside, which they will if we want them to, because they are mentally induced and therefore can, for the most part, be mentally reversed.

We create our own healing by becoming responsible, aware and compassionate with ourselves. As difficult as this can be, it is just what our dear, symptomized cells are urging us to do. Maturing in responsibility, emotional honesty and love can be a frustrating process at first, usually because we are ignorant of how to proceed and because we have so much emotional baggage repressed. But doing the psychological work necessary to know and free ourselves is certainly an easier way to live than not maturing. Our scar tissue is trying to tell us that.

CONCLUSION

The study of Body Symbolism is incredibly important. Talking to ourselves through our bodies is an experience as old as Humanity itself. And the joy of this New Age in history is that we now comprehend the importance of our Humanity and the dynamics of our body communication to a greater extent than ever before.

Operating in harmony with The Great Principle Of Reflectivity, we see that all ill conditions, whether achieved through disease or injury, are psychosomatic in nature. We also see that the *site* of the ill condition is not random, rather it is selected with great care to also serve as a communication from the inner us to the outer us.

A brief explanation here: motives for injury constructions can, but do not have to, include aspects not found in motives for disease construction. Inside an injury there is more "room" for beliefs of punishment, treachery, distrust of Life and people, denial of responsibility and victimhood to be operative. Each person gets to inspect and evaluate his personal and unique motives for choosing to injure himself, either alone or through cooperation with others.

Again, each and every negative condition and the site of that condition has a meaning, a specific belief-emotional root to it. We can profoundly benefit by understanding the code our minds use to communicate through our bodies. Obviously, as we learn to correctly assess the messages we give ourselves, we can more quickly comprehend our motivating belief-emotional states and then more effectively work to correct any internal imbalances. Thus, we can waste less energy, time and finances and experience much, much less pain, hassle and unhappiness.

My intent in writing this book is to assist in clarifying the existence of Body Symbolism and to assist in our decoding process. Some work has already been done concerning our body code, particularly in the ancient Chinese system of medicine and the work done by Carl Jung, Bio-energetics and Louise Hay (though I have not read her books). Some of the information that follows is known and some not yet well known. It is my intent to present this information so that it may be of practical use to us as we interact with ourselves, which we will always do because we are budding consciousnesses, committed to enlightened expansion. We have chosen to become physical again and be us for just that purpose.

I suggest when reading about the meaning of a particular ill condition you have experienced or are experiencing, ask yourself: "Could this explanation fit me?" If your answer is no, then what emotional meaning could you come up with for that condition? If your initial answer is yes, then what therapeutic change is indicated for you? How will you institute such a change? Create the atmosphere in your thought and emotion so you can learn and correct. Help yourself; do it with patience, do it with love.

CHAPTER TWO

BODY SYSTEMS

It is a basic premise of metaphysics that our universe is like a giant aquarium and we are all scuba-ing about our business. In order to enter, survive well and manipulate in our Earth environment, we put on bodies, diving suits of flesh and bone and assorted visceral accouterments. Each of us creates our own personal aquarium (TCTCHB) inside our Earth aquarium and our own body-diving-suit. We do this through the "magic" of thought, primarily at unconscious levels.

Here is an analogy of how this happens:

Our minds could be likened to a thirty story office building. We are usually aware of what is happening on the top six floors; they represent our Conscious Mind. Then there are two floors which are completely empty; no desks, no phones, no people; nothing. This represents the barrier of waking perception and repression. Then there are eight floors of our Subconscious Mind in which many outlandish events are happening. Our repressed, intense feelings are located here - - people are throwing things, there is hatred, there is sorrow, there is helplessness, happiness, there are orgies, there is intense fear and quite an assortment of consciously forgotten memories catalogued -- memories of every detail of every experience we have ever had (this incredibly includes all the advertisements ever seen, phone numbers ever dialed, names and dates ever learned and anything ever encountered). This is the layer of our mind hypnotists help us tap into when they suggest we remember "forgotten details" of an event or help us act like chickens on stage. Below these floors are fourteen floors which represent our Unconscious Mind. Our Unconscious Mind is a profound realm unto itself which contains immense energy that we are only beginning to understand. In these levels we are receiving phone calls and emotional visits from our previous Lives. We also receive messages from people in our current world through telepathic contacts, as well as communications from our Higher Self and other non-physical beings. In this level of our mind, we tend to our DNA codes and have access to realities we will experience in our future.

Also from our Unconscious Mind, operates the part of us which moment to moment creates all aspects of our world: our clothes, our rooms, our furniture, our spatulas, our houses, our plants, our animals, our people and so on. From these root floors, our Inner Self-consciousness, the all-knowing etheric director of our physical plan, creates and maintains our bodies far beneath the top floors of our waking awareness. This allows us the luxury of not having to concentrate on millions of minute, necessary details, like releasing enough thyroxin from our thyroid gland to stimulate cell metabolism. Thus, we are rather freed up on the surface so we can get on with the more interesting projects of Human consciousness, like learning how to love well, think well, be creative and have fun. So, our Inner Self takes a load off our Conscious Mind and creates our aura, a series of energy fields which mix and mingle and coalesce to form our body. This is a very smooth process, happens instantly, but not continuously; our bodies holographically blink on and off, but the offs are too brief for the crew on the top six floors of our mind to perceive it. They have other interests to tend to, so why bother with the blinking?

A Human body is a glorious, ever changing, buzzing, electronic vehicle we use to move around and manipulate inside this holographic Earth field. If we are going to be "here", we need to have a body.

Each body condition is a probable condition, chosen from a large number of probable conditions. No bodily state, "has to be", but each body state has to be chosen. Almost all body conditions are amenable to change if we so desire, excluding those conditions currently outside the framework of Humanness - - such as regenerating ears.

OUR EMOTIONS

Now that we have discussed the three-tiered nature of our mind (Conscious, Subconscious and Unconscious), let us discuss the nature of our emotions and hopefully clear up some common, Paradigm Two oriented misconceptions.

First of all, there are four basic components to a Human Being's mind: imagination, intuition, emotion and intellect. Again, imagination, emotion and intuition operate under the auspices of our feminine energy (PSYCHE) and our intellect operates through our masculine energy (TECHNE). Because we are all made of the same "stuff" as Goddess-God, we have more feminine energy than masculine energy. Imagination is our most powerful, creative attribute; emotion is the largest; intellect is the smallest and intuition runs through each of these to add tremendous depth and a sort of psychic sensuality to their use.

Paradigm One favored the development of emotion, intuition and imagination over the use of our intellect, whereas Paradigm Two has promoted intellect to the exclusion of the others. Paradigm Three favors advancement through the balanced use of all four psychic components. So, The New Age is this time in which we infuse emotional, imaginative and intuitive values, approaches and experiences into our currently overly-intellectual, distorted masculine energy culture. It is in the atmosphere of this powerful balance that we will create a new context in which to create a new self, then a new society, a new world and a New Age.

As mentioned, emotion is the largest component of Human nature. This is beautifully reflected in the way we have created our world in two spheres of activity: in the Earth and in our body. Of the four elements of our Earth (air, Earth, water and fire), the one that symbolizes emotion is water. Well, what percentage of our Earth's surface is covered with water? At least 66%. And what percentage of our body is comprised of water? At least 92%. How long can a person live without food? About six weeks. And how long can a person live without water? About three days. How much of our small intestine can we lose and still be ok? About 80%. Also, we could lose one lung, one kidney, every organ in our pelvis, our whole spleen and about 75% of our liver and still make it. But if we lose only 20% of our body's water, our body will die. So, how important are we symbolically showing ourselves water-emotion is to our inner nature, metaphysical livelihood and spiritual development? Crucial, at least.

In order to love ourselves better, to mature and develop our potentials, it would be helpful to understand the following dynamics concerning our emotional nature. First, contrary to a widely held, destructive belief, our emotions are not only caused by what happens to us. In essence, we feel the way we do because we think the way we do (Dr. Albert Ellis significantly increased our psychological understanding by first elucidating this "emotional mechanism" back in 1955 in his wonderful book, written with Dr. Harper, *A Guide To Rational Living*). We Humans think in terms of statements, questions and judgments; the ability to trigger an emotion rests with our judgments. "For me or against me and to what degree?" are the basic judgments we make. To create negative feelings about some event, we use negative judgments such as: "This is terrible, horrible or awful". Our thoughts may be either rational or irrational, accurate or inaccurate. Of course, we are better off making accurate, rational judgments about the events in our Lives, especially about ourselves (the primary event in our Lives). Too frequently we judge events as being terrible, horrible and awful when they really are not. We create overblown turmoil for ourselves when we could just judge the event as being yucky and leave it at that.

Another important concept about emotion is that there are two kinds of emotional pain on our planet, which I connote as being "normal" and "unnecessary" pains. "Normal" pain is a usual part of some unpleasant event, such as the pain of loss and grief we feel after the death of someone we love, the loss of a relationship, a job or a favorite object. I am sure we would all agree, there is enough "normal" emotional pain in Life without creating the "unnecessary" variety on top of it. Yet we do that to ourselves, over and over, when we think irrationally, misinterpret events or believe the multitude of ideas antithetical to the truth of life, which is love.

Also important to understand is that there are two aspects to emotions: creating them and expressing them. The basic rule of emotional health is: if we create an emotion, then we would do well to express that emotion, with harm to none. We will discuss expressing emotions more fully in Chapter Three.

It is wise, of course, to work to change our irrational thoughts into rational ones, thus creating less unnecessary pain. Thinking indeed can be irrational and inaccurate; emotions, however, never are. When some people begin the wise pursuit of monitoring and challenging their irrational thoughts, they sometimes make the mistake of dismissing the emotions crated by those thoughts, rather than dealing with them consciously. They erroneously think that because the thought was invalid, the emotion was too. Not so. <u>All</u> emotion is valid, whether created with irrational, inaccurate judgments or rational, accurate judgments. Once created, emotions ideally are to be respected and processed (i.e., felt and released) consciously.

Next, it is important to know that there are no "good" or "bad" emotions. There are emotions we do not enjoy too much and others we want to experience a whole lot more. Emotions of anger, sadness, despair, fear and terror case us to contract deeper into ourselves and shut others out. Emotions of love, compassion, gratitude and kindness cause us to want to expand and include others in our boundaries and hearts. We are dealing with expanding and contracting emotions, not good and bad feelings. We are here to learn how much we really prefer to feel the expanding emotions because they are so much more fun. We are also physical again to learn how to create the expanding emotions and stabilize into them most of the time.

Another important and little understood characteristic of emotion is that it is not affected by time. The old saying: "Time heals all wounds" (i.e., makes emotions go away), is totally false. In time, we may let go of hurts or repress them, but in no way does time itself operate to remove our feelings.

Another basic principle: there is no time in the realm of emotion. This means the pain, angers and fears we created and felt as children are still with us, unless we actively release them. If we could not be honest about our emotions when we were children (the case for most of us in our emotionally deprived society), then those early feelings are still in our emotional system, perhaps affecting us now.

Another characteristic of emotion is that, like everything else, it is energy and it accumulates; anger energy links up with anger energy, sadness with sadness, fear with fear and love with love. If we keep creating sadness, anger or fear and keep stuffing them inside us, we will accumulate larger and larger wads of energy until our system gets overloaded and overwhelmed, sometimes so much it just bursts! As mentioned, this is why many of us create disease or injury - - to both signal and help discharge the burdensome amounts of emotional energy we have built up.

Here is a nice analogy of these emotional principles currently being acted out in our Earth sphere. Just as there are streams and rivers under the surface of the Earth, so do our emotional systems flow under the surface of our Conscious Mind. When we stupidly dump toxic waste into the ground, it enters our water supply and pollutes it. Sometimes underground toxic wastes are carried downstream to pollute the drinking supply of a city far from the original dumping site. Well, in the same way anger that is dumped and dumped into our emotional river, say in childhood, can remain underground (i.e., out of awareness) and active for along time until a point in time when we accumulate and accumulate so much that it rises up to pollute future events, years downstream from the originating anger-events.

A final and very beautiful point metaphysics offers about emotions is this: we take them with us. The old saying: "You can't take it with you" only refers to material objects. When we die, since we are non-material beings, we take our non-material possessions with us; our imagination, intuition, thought and emotions. Our emotional nature, since it operates outside of time, is ours beyond time. This means the love and fulfillment we create this Lifetime are ours to keep forever. Any self-hate, guilt and shame, however, are ours, too, if we are hanging onto them when we die. They are all stored inside our Unconscious Mind, which connects us to all our Lifetimes.

If we want to maintain our emotional system in fine style, we must operate in harmony individually and culturally with the principles of our emotional Life just described. Recapitulated they are: 1) thinking creates emotion; 2) all emotion is valid; 3) if we create an emotion, then it is wise to express it; 4) always express emotions with harm to none; 5) it is wise to "uplevel" our thinking from irrational, inaccurate to rational and accurate, thus creating less unnecessary pain; 6) expanding emotions are more fun than contracting emotions; 7) there is no time in the realm of emotion; 8) emotion is energy; 9) emotional energy is cumulative 10) many of us give ourselves disease and/or injury to signal and help discharge emotional build-ups; and 11) when we die, we take our emotions with us.

As we become wiser in the truth of Human nature, we will be more able to live more healthfully. More on this as we go.

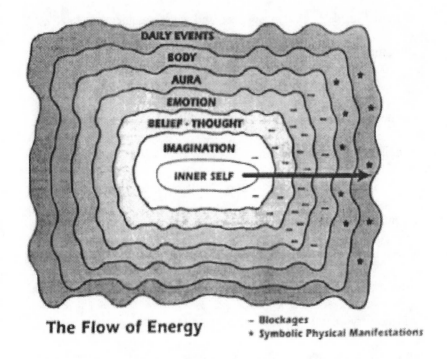

The Flow of Energy　　　－ Blockages
　　　　　　　　　　　　　　＊ Symbolic Physical Manifestations

Diagram

In this dazzling diagram, Ladies & Gentlemen, we see the progression of energy in the physical creation of our individual worlds. From our core spark of self, we send energy through our innermost spheres of activity outward to create our bodies and our world. If we have blockages in our inner levels (the negatives in the diagram), such as negative beliefs, negative thoughts or wads of repressed emotion, we will reflect these to ourselves through symbolic negative conditions in our outer layers, in our bodies and daily events (the asterisks in the diagram). The old saying: "What goes around comes around" aptly describes our interaction with The Great Principle Of Reflectivity. Indeed, we live our Lives from the inside <u>out</u>.

CAUTIONS

Before we get into the finer details of Body Symbolism, I want to raise a few issues of caution. First of all, we are going to discuss the general emotional dynamics operating in a person who chooses to give himself a disease or injury condition. Because we so much better understand the nature and mechanisms of our minds, we are becoming much more psychologically visible. Through understanding the mechanics and decoding of Body Symbolism, our emotional experience will be more and more revealed. Whereas people were previously much more of a mystery to themselves and each other, with increased awareness of metaphysics we will be able to better "read" the emotional events a person is creating and experiencing. Well, as Humanity expands and contacts more and more powerful concepts, the opportunity to use the new information in negative ways increases. As it relates to Body Symbolism, some people may want to play goofy, but common Negative Ego games with others' problems ("Gee, I don't have that condition. I guess I'm not as angry as you are. Hmmmm, I guess that shows I am more highly evolved and better than you."). Or, the person may take their anger out on someone and use a disease or injury condition as ammunition to punish (some version of: "Whatsa matter, you getting' sad? You gotta get sick? What a stupid decision; that's just like you!").

It is very important for each of us to realize that disease and injury conditions are purposeful and are, therefore, OK to have. In no way does physical or mental health indicate that a person is "better than" another. No one needs to feel ashamed or "less than" because we gave ourselves a disease or injury condition. If we need it, then it is our right to have it. Do not let anyone victimize us because of our selections. They are not in our shoes, our emotional world, so they do not know what is happening with us or the extent of what we are dealing with. They can't! Sometimes an illness is a wise choice - - a very wise choice. Please respect our inner-selection wisdom by refusing to allow others to hassle us unnecessarily. There is nothing "spiritually wrong" in having a health issue to work on.

And what is important for those of us who currently do not have disease or injury conditions or physical or mental handicaps, is to realize that we chose to share our worlds, sometimes personal and certainly societal and global, with people who do have them. Therefore, we are giving ourselves a message that people's handicaps, diseases and injuries (and their emotions) are important for our growth. Especially in regard that we need to be able to see beyond physical or emotional limitations and relate to The Being In Residence. I'm sure many ill, injured and handicapped people can chorus a resounding "Amen!" to that idea.

CHAKRAS

As mentioned in the overview of metaphysical principles in Chapter One, everything around us is comprised of energy, energy that is aware. This of course includes you and I (as well as our toothbrush, pens, coffee grinders, computers, etc.). It also is important to understand that there are <u>gradations</u> of energy and that

finer frequencies of energy can mix and merge, several times, to

create overlaid, denser frequencies of energy.

Our minds are very fine frequency systems which use

energy to create a thicker energy system of our auras, which then

create an even heavier energy clump of our bodies. Thus, our

bodies are clumpy energy fields existing within finer energy fields.

Modern physics with its increasingly sensitive instruments (and far-

sighted intuitions) has now caught up to this ancient knowledge.

Unfortunately, our Paradigm Two oriented medical science still lags

behind in comprehending and utilizing the truths and dynamics of

energy relationships, but they'll catch on pretty soon.

So, Humanity has established a system of energy transfer

from our consciousness to our auras, to our bodies. There are

locations in our bodies through which our Life force is infused from

the subtle realm of consciousness to the denser realm of body; these

points of energy infusion are called "chakras" (chakra is a Sanskrit

word meaning "wheel" (of energy)).

We can think of our consciousness as a tiny dot of light

which hovers about six inches above our head. According to some schools of metaphysics, our consciousness sends energy rays through the top of our head, down an etheric canal in the middle of our spinal cord to the lower chakra centers to be distributed to the rest of our body. This tiny canal in the middle of our spinal cord is the "sacred river" referred to in many mythologies of Eastern thought; it is analogous to the Jordan River of Palestine, the Ganges of India and the Nile of Egypt.

Our body's energy river branches at seven chakra centers to form tributaries that branch further as our beautiful Life force circulates throughout our bodies. These multi-branchings of energy are the meridian lines described and manipulated in Chinese acupuncture and in the very fine art of polarity therapy.

Chakras have been explored for thousands of years in Eastern cultures. There are several schools of approach that prescribe ways to work with and experience more directly the beautiful energies which animate our bodily and spiritual systems. The Hindu system, for instance, likens the chakra centers in shape, color and beauty to pulsing flowers of energy. The lower flowers are situated just in front of the spinal cord, the higher flowers are inside the brain and all will bloom when conscious thought is focused on them to purposely heighten their activity. This usually involves meditational exercises to elevate our Life energy from the first chakra at the base of our spine to the seventh chakra at the top of our head. This energy, however, can sometimes be unconsciously willed upward so that it feels like a surprise to us, sometimes even a traumatic surprise because the energy released can be so thunderously orgasmic. Through this experiential emersion in the sacred river of Life energy, a high form of spiritual baptism can take place. Great capacities for intense love, compassion, psychic abilities and wondrous, mystic experiences are said to be available to those who persist and succeed in purifying and elevating their Life energy into their "crown chakra."

Another importance of the chakra centers relates to the practical, day-to-day, minute-to-minute construction of our body as well as our growth issues. Each chakra affects its own area of the body, has its own psychological issue and own color. Chakra energies also directly affect our endocrine glands which are the main regulating and balancing system of our body. Let's examine our chakra centers individually.

Our first chakra (or wheel of energy) is located at the base of our spine. First chakra energy is related to security with self and the world - - concerns such as safety, food, shelter and personal worth. The color associated with our security center is red. Our next chakra is located in our genital area (affects ovaries and testes) and is concerned with creative sensual pleasure; taste, touch, smell, sight, hearing and sexual pleasure; its color is orange. Above this is our third energy center located in our stomach area (affects pancreas, spleen, liver, kidneys, stomach and adrenal glands). It is related to digesting, assimilating and releasing experience, particularly our contracting emotions, such as anger, sadness and fear; its color is yellow. Above this is our fourth chakra, the heart center (affects our thymus gland). It is designed to revel in the expanding emotions, such as love, joy, happiness, gratitude, peace and serenity. Our fifth chakra is located in our throats (affects our thyroid gland). Its energy is geared to the honest expression of self, especially our emotions; its color is blue. Our sixth chakra is located an inch above the bridge of our nose (affects our pituitary gland). It involves psychic growth; its color is indigo. Our seventh and highest chakra is located near the middle of our brain, behind and a bit down from the sixth chakra. This center is connected to our pineal gland; it is involved with metaphysical connections, bridges of energy and understandings to our higher consciousness and beyond; its color is violet.

Please note that the seven frequencies of energy used to create the body are intimately connected to our psychological issues of security, pleasure, contracting and expanding emotions, self-love, expression, intuition and awareness of more than the physical. Thus, the energies that create our body are the same energies that constitute our spiritual lessons; there is no division between the physical, mental, emotional and spiritual. Connected; whole.

GUIDELINES

To facilitate interpretation of our body messages, the following guidelines will help.

1) The last paragraph of the section on chakras is very important. This book will interpret the sites and types of disease and injury conditions by first relating to the chakra centers: "Which

chakra is involved?" and "Which psychological issue does that chakra represent?" are the initial questions to ask ourselves.

The first three chakras, having to do with security, pleasure, anger, fear, and sadness are the most physically oriented. The fourth and fifth chakras, having to do with love and honest verbal expression, are physical, but less so and serve as transitions between the material and spiritual realms. The highest chakra centers, the sixth and seventh, the pituitary and pineal, are oriented toward non-physical experience. When we interpret disease or injury to the head region, we would do well to consider the overall impacts of the condition to the body and the person's world.

2) We create bodily conditions according to principles of intuition and logic, so we use intuition and logic to interpret our body conditions.

3) There are several basic reasons why we give ourselves ill conditions; the following are the most common:

    A) Framework of Operation

    B) Bridge Framework

    C) Covert Gains

D) Symbols of Repressed Emotion

E) Punishments

F) Avoiding Creativity and Success

G) Ignorance

4) Our universe is energy-conservative in nature and we are all highly individualistic, so any body condition could have <u>one</u> or <u>several</u> meanings to it. It is our responsibility to evaluate each condition subjectively, as it pertains to <u>us</u> and our private emotional worlds. This book presents a general guideline to decoding bodily conditions; it does not present rigid definitions. We can use these ideas as a generalized map as we explore and interpret our very personal corporeal communications.

5) As mentioned in Chapter One, masculine and feminine energies are expressed in each person; the right side of our body expresses our masculine energies and the left side expresses our feminine energies. Therefore, a disease or injury affecting a body part on the right side of our body indicates a psychological issue related to our masculine energy, a man in our Life, men in general and/or our male energy dominated society. A negative condition placed on the left side of our body indicates a psychological issue

related to our feminine energy, a woman in our Life and/or women in general.

6) In summary, to best assess the reasons for creating unpleasant body conditions, ask ourselves these five questions:

> A) Which chakra is involved and what does it symbolize emotionally?
>
> B) What is the affected body part used for? What does its function symbolize emotionally?
>
> C) Did the body event occur on the right or left side?
>
> D) What happened because of the negative condition?
>
> E) What did not happen because of the condition?

Using our intuition and logic to answer these questions, we will best discern which directions to explore in decoding and understanding the communications hidden within our condition. Once we understand our messages, our prime effort then becomes reversing our mental/emotional motives with which we requisitioned the negative condition. At times this can be difficult, sometimes very difficult, but at least we now have an idea of what is going on through our bodies: <u>communication</u>. And now that we have some guidelines to interpreting our bodily messages, we can, if we desire, use this new knowledge to save ourselves years and tons of misery. How wonderful!

OUR BODY SYSTEMS

Let us now analyze the eleven basic organ systems of our body, what they represent psychologically and some possible motives for creating disturbances in their functioning.

OUR SKELETAL SYSTEM

We begin with our skeletal system because is the main structure of our body. Our skeleton serves as a living framework on and around which we arrange various visceral, neuronal and muscular organs, much as we would decorate a Christmas tree. Our skeletal system is made of bone, the second hardest living tissue. Besides bone, there are several varieties of connective tissue, all serving to support and hold our bodies together. Our bones also serve us by being a source of calcium ions for our blood and by forming needed blood cells.

It is interesting to note that many temples of spiritual worship in ancient cultures were comprised of three sections: the Outer Court, the Inner Court and the Innermost Court or the Holy of Holies. That architecture was patterned after our skeletal system, which serves as the design framework of our body temple. Our skeleton's pelvic girdle is analogous to the Outer Court. Our thorax, which houses our corporeal organs of fire - - our heart and lungs - - is analogous to the Inner Court and our wonderful cranium, which houses our brain with its most precious and powerful thought, is our Holy of Holies.

Psychologically viewed, the skeletal system represents the structure of our Lives; healthful, Positive Ego functioning of security, self-reliance and self-esteem. Our skeleton allows us to emotionally brace ourselves, to take a stand in Life, to support ourselves with security and pride. We hold ourselves up in the world with our skeletons, so we don't flop around like a peanut butter sandwich.

Disease or damage to our skeletal system indicates we are experiencing insecurity in supporting ourselves or that we feel the framework of our Life is fractured, eroding or crushed. Skeletal disturbance also occurs when we operate too much out of our "Negative Ego" rather than our "Positive Ego" (to be discussed more in Chapter Four).

OUR MUSCULAR SYSTEM

Our muscular system is a dual system, voluntary and involuntary, and is comprised of three types of muscle tissue: smooth, cardiac striated and skeletal striated. Smooth muscles are generally involuntary; they line the walls of organs with hollow cavities (esophagus, trachea, stomach and intestine) and serve to move food mass along the cavities. Next, cardiac striated muscle forms our heart, the most important muscle of our body. The third group, skeletal striated muscles, are attached to bones and are responsible for making our skeletons mobile. These muscles are voluntary and create the general shape of the body. They are most responsible for the beautiful, rhythmic, sensual movements Humans can enjoy as we engage in favorite, highly loving activities. There are approximately 310 muscles on each side of the body and, surprising to me, about one-fourth of a Human's muscles are located in the neck and face areas.

Muscle cells are characterized by their ability to contract to about one third their resting length. They respond to nerve, nerve-like or hormonal stimuli and are capable of great strength. Skeletal muscles in the lower part of our body are principally used for support and movement; they tend to be heavy in development. The skeletal muscles of our upper body tend to be softer and more pliable; available for quicker, more sensitive movements.

Psychologically speaking, muscles, especially skeletal muscles, represent a marvelous quality of consciousness: aggression. Muscle is designed to move us along the path of our Lives - - to aggress, to move, to take for ourselves what we want for a growth-filled Life. Muscles, therefore, represent our sense of personal power and self-reliance.

It is noteworthy that kids who feel a lack of power, often because of a deprivation of love and too much fear, often compensate as they age by over-developing their skeletal muscles. Wilhelm Reich called this compensatory use of muscle tissue "character armor". Such a person, starting in his teens or 20s, encases himself in a hard, almost inflated suit of muscle to present an image as a mightily powerful person and thus ward off anticipated attack. Using muscles as character armor, however, has definite adverse effects on our emotional/spiritual growth. Chronically tough, tense muscles will decrease the all-important quality of sensitivity; frozen muscles block emotions and intuitions, thus keeping our true feelings out of awareness. This, of course, only perpetuates the condition the person felt originally: that of self-alienation which, of course, limits how much we can love ourselves, which definitely limits true personal power.

Damage to muscles through disease or injury usually represents concerns about aggression and personal power, often because of a belief in weakness, an immense fear of, or a stubborn unwillingness to be, self-reliant. Negative conditions in muscles that are severe can indicate a desire to stop movement in one's Life and even a desire to go backward in time and development to lost, bygone days of perceived protection and acceptance (more on this in Chapter Four).

OUR SKIN SYSTEM

Our beautiful skin is the heaviest organ of our body, having an average weight of about six pounds. Skin is a multi-layered organ which serves the five fine functions of: <u>absorbing</u> nutrients and oxygen, <u>excreting</u> water and carbonic gas, <u>regulating</u> body temperature through perspiration, <u>protecting</u> against invasion by micro organisms, chemicals and ultraviolet light and, finally, <u>sensing</u> the environment (hot, cold, pressure, pain and pleasure).

Also, our skin contains "ocelli", which are cells with many tiny nerve endings. These ocelli are light sensitive and seem to function as primitive, but effective, sensing organelles similar in structure to the cells in our retina. Several experiments have been recorded (including a *"Sixty Minutes"* Episode) in which blind and blindfolded people were taught to "see" using their skin. These ocelli organelles are reported to be concentrated in the forehead (sixth chakra, "third eye" area), chest, palms and, even, the back of our head (re: "eyes in the back of her head").

In his books, *"Seth Speaks"* and *"The Nature Of Personal Reality"*, Seth related two other exciting and important operations of the skin. This may seem far out to some, but Seth says the skin in a pregnant woman's abdomen has the ability to open up in such a way as to allow a spirit-inhabited-fetus an opportunity to look out at his new world and orient himself to his surroundings as he begins another Lifetime. Another very important function of skin is to serve as a doorway through which emotions can flow. The nature of emotion, you see, is that it, like the lasagna we ate a day ago, wants to flow <u>through</u> us. Otherwise, the wad of energy gets stuffed inside us, into our aura, where it stagnates. Seth says that whenever we feel a strong emotion we release it along with certain "mental enzymes", which flow through our skin into the air. This means that just as there are cold fronts in the air, so are there "anger fronts" and "fear fronts". And, yes, emotional fronts then go on to mix and merge on a larger scale to create our weather. Because we create our TCTCHBs, we and others create, in a "mass event" way, our sunny or rainy days, tornadoes, droughts, hurricanes and ice storms. For example, when feeling very fearful, we may create a severe cold spell, complete with a heavy accumulation of society-stopping snow, to "put the freeze on" our reality so it does not progress and then we do not have to face what we fear. Also, sometimes when we feel we are drowning on our emotions, we collectively conspire to create a flood. Yep, we create our total experience in this Lifetime's TCTCHB, on micro and macro scales. Incredible ideas, eh? Imagine how interesting it would be if we could visibly color our emotional enzymes and actually see what we're walking around emitting? Some psychic people have that experience when they read auras.

Psychologically speaking, because skin is our outermost layer, the part of us we first present to the world, it represents our image of ourselves. Our self-image is the attitudinal picture of ourselves we look through moment to moment, much like wearing eyeglasses. Our self-image is comprised of our core beliefs about ourselves, as well as our feelings for ourselves, both conscious and, especially, unconscious. Metaphysically, we continually manifest our self-image all around us in our TCTCHBs; in essence, we live in a self-image reality.

Those who have damaged or erupted skin are giving ourselves a communication about how we see ourselves in relation to a personal issue. Skin eruptions on our left hand, for example, have different meanings than eruptions on our right foot. Our self-image may seem to be ok and may appear just fine to others, but unconsciously we may not really fee that way (perhaps because of shame or inferiority) and thus use our skin to communicate.

OUR DIGESTIVE SYSTEM

Our digestive system is a marvel of corporeal engineering; most organs of our body play a part in our fueling process. Using food for our physical livelihood involves two complicated processes: 1) digestion, which is the breaking down of food mass into its nurturing components and 2) absorption, which is the intake of these components and their transfer (feeding) to the cells themselves.

The digestive process begins in our mouth with the secretion of saliva. Digestion continues a bit in our stomach and occurs primarily in the duodenum, the first part of our small intestine. Here proteins are broken down into amino acids, fats are changed into glycerides and carbohydrates are metabolized into glucose. These nutritional elements are then absorbed in our small intestine, which winds around and around a length of about twenty feet inside our abdomen, giving any food mass a heavy absorptive going over. Then when we are done processing the chow in our small intestine, we send it for one last work-over to our five foot long large colon, making sure we absorb maximum benefit from our food.

Unlike other Life forms in other realms of existence, much of a Human's physical security depends on the procurement, eating, digestion and absorption of food. On many other levels, beings are not physical so they do not have bodies that require food. And if they do create a body-form to relate through, it still doesn't require food, unless they want to eat; perhaps a small salad. We Humans are so into food because it is an important Earth symbol for what we need the most for our livelihood and growth, which is spiritual nourishment. Our need for our dearly beloved food groups, which is satisfied through the conscious, loving cooperation of our mineral, plant and animal neighbors, is symbolic of our daily minimal spiritual requirements of love, truth, hugs, meaning and destiny.

I am sure you have heard the medical maxim which encourages us to chew each bit of food thirty two times before we swallow it. The purpose of this maxi-mastication is to thoroughly break down the food morsel, thus making it easier for our systems to accomplish digestion. Similarly (and this is a very important point), we are encouraged to break down each moment-morsel of our Life experience with awareness and thought (chewing analogs to analyzing). Thus, we may more easily digest (comprehend) the truth of our emotional experience and then absorb that experience-food to spiritually nourish ourselves into higher levels of growth and higher levels of love.

Difficulties in our third chakra digestive system, ranging from a sour stomach to nausea, to ulcers, to colitis, to a colostomy indicate an emotional imbalance resulting from difficulty in digesting and assimilating some aspect of our emotional experience, usually because it is so hurtful to us. It is as if we are having a hard time processing in our guts some wad of fear, sadness, anger, disappointment, guilt, etc. So it sits there and "eats away" at us.

It is interesting to note that some of us may also give ourselves digestive difficulties to signal our unprocessed, unfelt positive emotions. These are the people who refuse to look at the bright side of Life, or who have built our identities around being victims, never quite making it or only being good at coping with hardship and complaining and complaining. Our emotional imbalance is such that our positive, expansive emotions are repressed and then stagnate in our guts.

OUR EXCRETORY SYSTEM

Our excretory system serves the crucial functions of removing digested matter, undigested matter and toxicity from our systems. The waste products of metabolism are excreted in solid, liquid and gaseous forms.

As consciously evolving entities, Humanity has set about to learn the art of <u>consistent</u> <u>creativity</u>. We learn this crucially important experience through interaction with and improvement upon the feedback field of Earth Life. As we nourish our bodies with food and release the toxins from food processing, so are we to spiritually nourish ourselves with daily events and then release the "toxins" of a digested (fully understood, fully felt) emotional experience. Psychologically speaking, our excretory system reflects how we relate to emotional toxicity, i.e. repressed emotion, particularly denied frustration, pity, sorrow, guilt, sadness, rage and fear. Our excretory system functions under the influence of third chakra energies.

As discussed in Chapter One, our current Paradigm Two oriented society has several rules and regulations, mostly based on superstition, against feeling and displaying emotion. Our societal sanctions of how to get love and acceptance still require a "controlled" demeanor, a repressive approach to our inner world. People actually apologize for weeping on TV when they are discussing a traumatic event or a wonderfully touching event! We are so encouraged to reject our imagination and repress our emotions (particularly fear, sadness and anger) that, after a while, some of us cannot take it anymore and just explode. This is the chief cause of digestive and excretory problems (also strokes). On societal and global levels, unprocessed, unreleased emotions explode as violence, riots and natural disasters.

The key to maintaining a healthful balance of expanding and contracting energies in our systems is to continually experience our emotions bit-by-bit and to release them bit-by-bit. Unfortunately, we are still rather unpracticed at coping with anger and hate, often believing the destructive myth that these feelings lead to violence. Actually, anger and hate are innocent. If left alone and released as felt, in gradations, they would just pass through our skin like so much perspiration. But instead we hold them in. We stockpile them and let them fester. Worst of all, many of us still believe in violence.

Then, when we have enough repressed emotional force behind this disgusting, ugly belief, we act harmfully. Then we deflect responsibility and say: "The anger/hate made me do it"; "crimes of passion" and all those ridiculous rationalizations.

Imagine how you would feel if you carried in your intestines twenty years of unreleased excretory material. Well, that is exactly how many of us are relating to our emotional systems; we are repressing our earliest sorrow for hurts received, hates for hurts received and rage for our hurts. I want to emphasize that these painful emotions result from frustrating the most basic desire of every Human Being: to give love and receive love. In light of this, please analyze what happened when you were growing up. How did you feel about it? How did you process your feelings? Are you still carrying around a sack full of hurts, angers and fears? It is so very ironic: we carry these feelings around because we are trying so hard to hide from them at the same time. We want to hide from our hurt, sadness and rage so we deny them and stuff them into our invisible knapsack, our aura. The emotions we repress "hang there", as it were, out of our awareness so that we lug them around, with all their harmful effects, into everything we do.

Well, how are you feeling now? What is in your emotional knapsack, your guts? Are you emotionally clear with your memories? If not, you likely have some "toxins" yet to excrete. Better do it emotionally before you symbolize it physically.

Spiritual development, as befits any consciously evolving entity, requires that we ventilate our emotional storehouse to keep our growth fresh. But we must vent our emotions "with harm to none" or else it is not spiritual and there is no growth.

Here is an example of processing and releasing the "toxins" from a bit of Life experience, as we would release the toxins from processing a bit of food:

Let us say I phone a woman I have recently met and invite her to have lunch with me. She replies that she would really like to, but has a busy schedule this week and would like me to call her next Monday to make arrangements for that week. I agree, we chat briefly and then say goodbye. Ok, so now the big question: how do I feel? Well, most of me feels happy that she wants to be with me and has accepted my invitation. On the other hand, I also make myself feel a little rejected - - I extended myself to her and she said no. I also feel a little frustrated because I did not get what I wanted. Hmmm, I also created a bit of anger because I am telling myself she wants to play hard to get. Well, upon examination, that last thought is irrational, based on scanty evidence and a trace of sexism, so I will change it to give her the benefit of positive intent, assume she is being honest and wait to see what happens next week. Ok. Now, Richard, let go of the feeling of rejection (phew), release the frustration (phewww) and let go of the irrationally created anger (phewwww). Really release them, ok? (phewww). Yep. Ok, Richard, now let's go to the next bit of our Life experience, taking no unfinished emotional business from the previous one with us.

And keep working to cut loose that damn sexism! Thanks very much, amen.

For many of us the issue then arises: "Why, if I had to analyze and parcel out each and every feeling I had about each and every damn bit of experience I have in the course of an hour, let alone a whole day, why I would never get anything done." Actually, processing emotionally does not take forever, is not impractical and we will be much better serving our spiritual well-being.

Imagine saying to your boss: "Sorry I didn't get the Rybicki reports done, but I had to process out a rejection from Kathy and a hurtful, repressed-anger-motivated jab from Tony. Then there was another power-tripping-gambit from that creep Arnold and that took me twenty minutes to sort it all out. I really felt angry because it pushed a button of what my father used to pull on me that I have obviously not cleared out yet. I'm truly sorry, Boss, and I sure hope you understand. If not, I'll have to process that out and it will take me even longer to get the damn report done!"

This may be exaggerating a little, but only a little. In the beginning of practicing awareness and analyzing, we may find the going a bit tedious and frustrating, but as we free ourselves up emotionally and become more adept at processing our experience, we will be able to zip along without cumbersome delays.

Please remember that The Great Principle Of Reflectivity requires that the more we want to have a wonderful outer world, the more we must tend to and straighten up our inner world. This is the major responsibility which comes with the beautiful gift of Free Will. The sooner we act in harmony with this central truth of consciousness, i.e., responsibility, the sooner we will give ourselves the abundant, fun-filled reality we want. We will also be better able to learn the intense joy of worshipping love, truth and beauty as well as keeping our excretory systems in good shape.

OUR RESPIRATORY SYSTEM

To me, oxygen is one of the most beautiful experiences of being Human. I mean, I love oxygen; I would marry it if I could. In effect, we each do when we first inhabit our bodies (usually by the seventh month of gestation).

Oxygen is carried to each of the trillions of cells in our body at an incredible rate. On our deepest cellular levels we need oxygen. Oxygen assists in the inbreath of energy, the infusion of animating Life essence from our mind into our body. In fact, oxygen is so closely linked with energy transfer and the refinement of energy, that the Hindu culture has developed several effective systems of yoga breath control as aids in meditation and mystic experience. This ancient art is being updated a bit by the Breathing Movement which encourages styles of breathing to help discover and release emotional blockages, some of which we may have started while we were still in or just leaving the womb.

Our ecosystem also centers around oxygen, with key supporting roles being played by carbon, nitrogen and hydrogen. The animal kingdom is the first level of Earth consciousness to depend on oxygen for physical sustenance. In the Human kingdom, consciousness has created a system of processing and distributing oxygen that is more suitable to the requirements of higher mind development. We have given ourselves a heavy duty lung system which will nourish our cells with oxygen and release carbonic gas into the atmosphere which then goes to help our little buddies in the plant kingdom who, of course, help us immensely by creating the oxygen we are so dependant upon in the first place. How lovely and delicate our balance in Nature! Too bad we are so out of balance with our emotional truths that we still so cruelly attack our neighbors in our ecosystem the way we do.

Psychospiritually speaking, involvement with breath represents involvement with Life. Breath is the great harmonizer; it physically charges our cells and our nervous systems. Breath is intimately connected to the flow of energy coursing through our bodies; reduced, shallow breathing leads to reduced emotional experience, which leads to low energy in our body, which often leads to not feeling powerful or safe. Breathing patterns change when different emotions are released through the skin; gasping accompanies fear, sobbing accompanies sorrow and short, snorting breaths accompany intense anger.

Difficulties in our respiratory system indicate emotional fatigue caused by large amounts of emotion stuffed inside us. Outwardly, we may be dealing with distressing events, such as tragedies, domination, heavy expectations or violent punishments.

Inwardly we may feel like we are drowning or suffocating in sadness, anger or fear. It is as if we have a difficult time dealing with air because we have no "room to breathe" emotionally. And sometimes we get so angry we do not breathe well - - it is as if our "Child Within" is not getting his way (i.e. being loved) and he is defiantly holding his breath, waiting for the outside situation to change. We will discuss some lung-related conditions in the following chapters.

OUR CIRCULATORY SYSTEM

Our circulatory system is comprised of three basic aspects: our heart, our blood vessels and our blood. We will consider these aspects in two groups: heart with blood vessels and then blood.

Our heart is ruled by the fourth chakra energies, those energies concerned with the root experience of all Life everywhere: love. The fourth chakra serves as the boundary between material and spiritual concerns.

Basically, disturbances of the heart are related to concerns of the heart. This is no surprise to you, I am sure, because this is ancient knowledge reflected in common phrases such as: "heartfelt thanks", "heart in hand", "affairs of the heart", "speaking from my heart", "wearing my heart on my sleeve", "my heart cries for you", "cold hearted", "heartbreak hotel", "with an open heart", "hard hearted, rotten creep", "died of a broken heart", etc.

Our heart is the doorway to spiritual illumination, the path each seeker, each winner, must walk to discover our Life's true meaning and joy. Those who choose this enlightening path expand their heart into health and radiant illumination. Whereas those who unfortunately walk in self-alienation, self-dislike, emotional repression and/or violence, constrict their hearts into pain and often disease.

The classic book by Doctors Friedman and Rosenman, *Type A Behavior And Your Heart*, describes a correlation of a hard-driven, super-achievement-race-against-time personality with heart problems. Some people who are Type A are living in harmony with their personality and have no heart problems. Those who are not authentic Type As and feel pressured to live as such, are the ones who are likely to manifest cardiac problems. People who continually treat themselves in an uncaring, unbalanced fashion often do not feel their own love or the love of others or the love Life itself has to offer. They are too busy achieving and producing, most often to prove their Inner Worth, which is impossible.

Usually they are also making their own love conditional: "After I make a million bucks (and prove my father right/wrong), then I will slow down (and like myself - - maybe)." These unfortunate people are too materialistically busy, too outside controlled to allow themselves time to feel. This is so sad because a primary truth about love is that it is very sensual and sensuality requires a leisurely approach. Love requires concentration; the more one savors it, the more love expands. Feminine Energy (love) cannot be railroaded (dominated) into place; it has to be invited and then wined and dined. And felt grateful for. And explored and known and then known deeper (that can take a while). And then felt grateful for again. And celebrated. And then, eventually, love has to be loved. So, what's with all the rushing?

Heart difficulties, whether achieved through disease or injury, can secondarily symbolize disappointment and anger at not being loved enough by others (wherein we feel our heart has been attacked). Heart problems can also be created and used to manipulate someone else into acting more kindly ("I've gotta have a heart attack before you stop being mean to me?").

Next, blood, psychologically speaking, relates to family. "Blood ties" and "blood lines" are old expressions meant to remind us of what is thicker than water.

Creating a difficulty with our blood is generally meant to convey an emotional problem in relating to our family. This could also be symbolic of difficulty in relating, on a larger level, to the Family of Mankind. "Difficulty in relating" usually translates into feelings of lack of love and concomitant pain and anger.

Blood pressure relates to our emotional balance. When we elevate our blood pressure, we are indicating we are out of balance - - too much pressure, too much energy (emotion) locked up in our system so that our circulation is speeding, rushing, running too fast. When we lower our blood pressure, we signal being out of balance in the direction of withdrawal of energy; depression, lethargy, resignation and perhaps giving up.

Because arteries and veins run through and affect our entire body, they are multi-faceted in function and meaning. Therefore, there is no clear cut definition to their symbolism. In deciphering blood vessel problems, consider the chakra, the function of the body part affected and the impact of that body part. A blood clot in a leg, for instance, will indicate something different from a blood clot in the brain. Then again, it may not; it depends on the private world and personal style of the person so afflicted. Once again, I stress the need for individual, subjective evaluation. I will clarify sites of blood clots and injuries in the next chapter.

OUR REPRODUCTIVE SYSTEM

With our finely tuned reproductive systems, Humanity provides itself three accomplishments: one, we allow ourselves the beautiful experience of creating the physical conditions necessary so that another spirit may inhabit a physical body. Two, using our sexual organs wisely, we can allow ourselves and others great pleasures from loving sexual communication, which can lead to increasing spiritual awareness, which in turn can lead to greater love and security. The third service of our reproductive system is that it anchors our sexual identification, it being an organic symbol of our inner choice to act out this Lifetime as a female or male.

Because our sexual organs are ruled by second chakra energies, they are powerful pleasure centers. Coming out of a framework of Paradigms One and Two, this has quite understandably led to much attention and a whole lot of abuse being placed on our reproductive systems throughout history, with women getting an exceptionally heavy dose. Our current generations have become rather fixated on second chakra functioning. One reason for this is that preceding generations have denied openly exploring our pleasure and sexual natures. Another reason being that we are still rather afraid of moving up and dealing with the next level of our development, our third chakra issues of handling our contracting emotions. Thus, many of us do not yet know the hurt and angry parts of ourselves, feel insecure about them and therefore heap all kinds of non-sexual, non-pleasure experiences onto our sexuality (S&M is a good example of this).

Because we tend to so emotionally deprive ourselves, we use our reproductive system (more than the other systems of our body) to manufacture a sense of phony security, phony self-esteem and phony power. Our egos fixate on the size or our organs and glands, on the number of orgasms and on the number of similarly fixated egos who are fixated on our glands. "They can't get enough of my glands" is still a common passport to societal thrills of cheap popularity.

It seems that we are increasingly being programmed by advertising, movies, television and books into identifying men and women's worth with our body's physical condition. In particular, we are merchandizing women's appearances as we merchandize refrigerators. This is not a random comparison; our TECHNE, masculine-energy-dominated, Paradigm-Two-oriented, patriarchal society is emotionally cold and many of us wind up treating ourselves and others as objects (no emotions - - outside focus only; pull the handle, enter a cold space).

In coping with these deadening, anti-emotion, anti-Life influences, we can create tremendous distress in our guts. Our reproductive systems often become the site of manifesting emotional conflicts about sexual expectations and treatment. It is interesting to note that men seem not to create quite as many reproductive difficulties as do women. In our culture men are programmed, on the one hand, to overvalue in a bravado sort of way sexual organs as a statement of male worth. On the other hand, men are taught that our worth depends even more on our monetary and social status. So, to communicate anger messages about sexual oppression, men often attack financial security and social standing more than sexual organs (although men are increasing the frequency of prostate cancer). Disease conditions in a male's reproductive system usually result from feeling tired and angry from lack of fun, pleasure and nurturing (second chakra) because of too much wasted time playing the stereotype Big Protector, Iron Man role (the military, wrestling and "tough" guys well model this game).

Women seem to more freely give themselves disease conditions in their reproductive systems. The prime emotional motive behind these conditions ("female problems") has to do with anger at what it has meant to them to be a woman in our culture. This is where the horrible effects of at least twenty one centuries worth of sexism and cruelty come to "bear" - - on the reproductive organs. Many women's anger sounds something like this: "People (mom, dad, society) think being a female is not important and have treated me cruelly. I feel enraged about the less-than limitations and hurts repeatedly put on me! My femaleness (as biologically defined by my ovaries, fallopian tubes, uterus, vagina, clitoris and breasts) is what attracted this terrible treatment to me, so that is where I will locate my (communication) condition."

Another motive for sexual organ distress in women has to do with the intense pressure put on women to bear children. Our societal stereotype dictates that women who do not have children are only half-women, that something is dreadfully wrong with them and that a childless woman can never be fulfilled and happy. This rancid message is decreasing with the enlightenment of the Women's Movement, but is still operative to an alarming degree. Also, this prejudice can piggyback on a woman's true desire to have and raise children.

To illustrate the above paragraph, it is interesting to note that cancer of the endometrium, which is the membrane which lines the uterus, most often occurs in women who are post-menopausal and have had no children. Because of sexual stereotypic beliefs and pressures put on women to prove their worth as a Human by proving their worth as a woman (i.e. proving their worth as a baby-bearer), and perhaps because of frustration of her own healthful desires to have children, a woman past child bearing age can feel awfully angry at herself and circumstances and can also feel very guilty. Sounds something like: "I did not validate myself by validating my womanhood. I did not even achieve the standards my mother did. And I gypped myself out of a very beautiful, loving experience; I really wanted to feel the special closeness of a healthy mother-child relationship and now I never will. I am a failure. I hate myself and I hate "them" for telling me to hate myself. I think I will punish myself." Because of a desire to appear "strong", these feelings and their intensity can be, and often are, repressed. That is why the reproductive system is unconsciously chosen to relay the emotional message upstairs, to our Conscious Mind. Closely aligned to cancer of the endometrium, but much less severe, is endometriosis, a condition chosen frequently these days. Endometriosis is often referred to as the "career woman's disease" because single, childless professional women who are committed to their careers seem "somehow prone" to the condition. This is understandable because as our beginning generations of career women increasingly choose work over motherhood, they can run into heavy conflicts with their old, Paradigm One-Two programming. These women may want their careers, but feel guilty about it or they may not really want their careers, but feel stuck with them (either to prove something or because they are not allowing themselves other experiences). Either way, as reflected in the increasing incidence of endometrial and reproductive disorders, women seem to be increasingly angry about these oppressions.

The key to untangling these heavy emotional knots is for women and men to work to let go of all sexist beliefs ("men are better than women"; "women are better than men"), separate arbitrary sexual stereotypes from our true desires, express and release anger at the opposite sex (starting with mom, dad), work to forgive her, him, them and then get on with living Life creatively, as a true woman or man, a true self. This may take a lot of work for some of us, but the rewards are sure worth it. We will discuss other concerns of the reproductive system in Chapters Three and Four.

OUR NERVOUS SYSTEM

The Human nervous system is the most intricate and complex of all "living" mechanisms ("living" is in quotes because our general definition and awareness of aliveness is still rather limited; science and society have generally not understood nor accepted that the atoms which comprise the clothes you are now wearing are living and aware, let alone the multitude of beings alive on the multitude of other dimensions of consciousness).

Our nervous system is comprised of a brain, a spinal cord and nerve networks. Nerve impulses are conducted from the periphery of our body and organs to the central nervous system (CNS) and from the CNS back to our body organs and periphery. Thus, our nervous system serves to connect our consciousness to the outer world and connect our consciousness to our inner, body world. In order to best accomplish this, Humanity has designed two complimentary nervous systems, the voluntary and the autonomic. The voluntary system is how our consciousness connects to and manipulates our external environment; it functions according to the power of our will. The autonomic system is divided into two aspects, both feminine energy in nature; the sympathetic and parasympathetic. The sympathetic nervous system is in charge of the autonomic reactions concerned with fight or flight reactions (increasing respiration, sweating, stopping digestion of food, increasing circulation to skeletal muscles, etc.). Our parasympathetic nervous system is concerned with the hour-to-hour monitoring and regulating of our body's internal environment. Nerves have their most direct impacts upon our brain and muscles.

The way our Earth system operates, the more evolved a consciousness is, the more developed is its body's nervous system. Also, the more evolved the consciousness, the more it will place its nervous system near the surface of its body. The contrast is often made between a crayfish and a Human; the crayfish is "shelled-in", whereas a Human's outsides are soft, our skeletal system is inside and much of our nerves are peripheral. The hallmark of a developing, maturing consciousness, you see, is sensitivity; our nervous system allows us intense sensitivity to both our external and internal worlds.

Imagination is the root ability of Human consciousness, which then branches into five aspects: our will, our intuition, our emotion, our intellect and our body creation. It is through the vast, yet unrealized power of imagination that all creation everywhere, in all dimensions of Life, flows. Our non-physical, imagination-based identity greatly relies upon our nervous system to anchor itself to and operate in physical reality, chiefly through our brain.

Only our chakra system is more intimately involved in processing Life energy than is our nervous system. Our nervous system specifically deals in the transfer and interpretation of energy modulation. As such, our brains are nests of lightening storms, continually sparking as the finer frequencies of thought, emotion and intuition zing and sing their electrical songs within us.

There are, according to Lazaris, Seth and several other authors, areas of our brains we still do not use. Many experiences are still open to our evolution as Humanity expands into our fulfillment. Seth says there are untapped areas of our brains that will allow us to see sound, hear color and sense the past and future around people and objects.

Because nerves affect the entire body, disturbances in the nervous system must be interpreted according to the chakra area and body functions affected. Because nerves deal with perception and will and greatly affect muscles, nervous system disturbances generally indicate dilemmas about perception, personal power and self-reliance. Nervous system dysfunctions generally suggest a desire to not be aware of and connected to the outside world; the person feeling "I can't take it anymore!" and wanting to draw a perceptual shade. The emotions behind these conditions are generally frustration, sorrow, fear, sadness and, of course, intense anger.

OUR ENDOCRINE SYSTEM

Our endocrine system is a glandular system which regulates through chemical means (hormones) the activation or inhibition of several important organs and system. As such, the endocrine system is often referred to as the Great Regulator And Balancer of body conditions, the system most in charge of maintaining stable and harmonic states of health. The endocrine glands, from top down are: the pineal, the pituitary, the thyroid, the parathyroids, the thymus, the pancreas, the adrenals and the ovaries/testes. Endocrine glands are located in each chakra center and are the physical correlates of them; they are therefore incredibly sensitive to thought and emotion.

Psychologically speaking, endocrine disturbances are best interpreted like neuronal disorders: by analyzing the chakra area and the practical function of the body part affected. This is especially important in de-coding negative conditions of the pituitary and pineal glands because they are so etheric they do not hold much meaning in themselves, but more so in the effects obtained by manipulating them.

For instance, a disturbance placed in the anterior lobe of the pituitary gland can cause the cortex of the adrenal gland to increase secretion of male hormones, called androgens. Characteristic of this situation is increased male qualities of the body; excessive hair growth on legs, abdomen and face, increased muscle development in shoulders, enlarged penis or clitoris and a deeper voice. If the person who creates this syndrome is a woman, it may indicate that she feels angry or fearful about being a woman and feels the only way out of her oppression is to adopt the physical characteristics of the "top dog", male sex. Whereas, if the person is a male, this condition may indicate an insecurity about his maleness, such that he feels he has to take on an overbearing masculine appearance to compensate for inner feelings of lack.

As you can see, endocrine functioning has far reaching effects on our body's condition. A similar system of our body, which many physiologists would categorize as a sub-system of our endocrine system, is our immune system.

OUR IMMUNE SYSTEM

When we discuss the dynamics of disease in our bodies, we indirectly acknowledge the opposite polarity, which is our body's physical defense against disease, our immune system. This body system is what our mothers and grandmothers often referred to as our "resistance". "Keeping our resistance up" was considered to be a holy mission, which they undertook with ardent fervor, usually through intense ministrations of castor oil, chicken soup, hot ginger ale and encouraging the "right" amount of sleep (i.e. dreaming).

Our immune system operates to maintain a homeostatic balance in our body by gobbling up pathogens such as bacteria, viruses or fungi that threaten our body's well-being. The major element of our immune system is our white blood cells (called lymphocytes), which are manufactured in our lymph glands. These cells are our body's "soldiers" which neutralize pathogens; the resulting gooey blend of pathogen and expended lymphocyte is what we call puss.

No other system of our body is receiving as much attention in current medical research as is our immune system. Because of the heavy impacts of our brain's hypothalamus (which processes emotion) on our endocrine system, which then goes to heavily influence our immune system, more research is being directed to studying the interplay of emotional stress and resistance to disease. Indeed, we are discovering that through psychological reactions and conditioning, we can either increase or decrease our immune response. For instance, researchers have found that through the distress of capture, big horn sheep reduce their level of lymphocytes for an average of two months; similarly, Humans often decrease our immune response during the first two months after the death of a spouse.

These and other demonstrations of the impacts of emotion on "resistance" are leading to a wonderful awakening that is reversing much of our Paradigm Two bias of traditional immunological thinking. As stated in Chapter One, a new area of medical science has been established to study the interdependence of psychology and the immune system called Psychoneuroimmunology.

Psychologically viewed, our immune system symbolizes our desire to fight for ourselves. Our immune system is created and maintained under the aegis of our masculine energy and our will. Disease or injury resulting in or from poor immunological functioning generally indicates beliefs and feelings of weakness, depression, an overload of anger, and in extreme instances, a feeling of giving up and not fighting for ourselves. The condition called Acquired Immune Deficiency Syndrome (AIDS) is a good example of this type of disorder.

There are other disease conditions in which the immune system behaves in an opposite manner; it revs up and actually attacks parts of our own body. These diseases are called auto-immune disorders and they, with their psychological motives, are discussed in Chapter Four.

REINCARNATION AND HEALTH

As mentioned in Chapter One, we give ourselves the benefit of many Lifetimes to learn our lessons in Earth school. We try to cram as many varied, intense experiences into as brief a span as we are able to. What in Earth terms is one hundred twenty five thousand years of Earth Lives is a wonderful immersion in a pool of warm, growing wisdom in Soul terms. Many times we enter, are born and seek to get our learning right. How kind we are to ourselves to allow so much research and depth in our evolution through Earth school explorations.

With respect to health, some people who research the dynamics of reincarnation suggest that our "previous" Lifetimes can cause our current set of experiences or problems and if we could become aware of the "previous" hurts our current condition would disappear ("previous" is in quotes because all our Lifetimes are occurring at once, outside of time, though they each have time inside them. Thus, no Lifetime occurs before or after any other; they are all happening right now, inside the spaceless, timeless totality that is our Soul, our total self).

Many people have indeed freed themselves from health problems by resolving emotional issues from other Lifetimes. I have seen it happen, as have many researchers and reputable hypnotherapists.

In order to understand how this can occur, it is important to remember that our mind is an open system. As mentioned in the analogy of our mind as a thirty story office building, our Unconscious Mind is connected to all our Lifetimes and can access any information from anyone else we have ever been, including their strengths, fears and unresolved growth issues.

Reincarnation comes into play in these ways: sometimes we have a growth issue we did not work through in other Lifetimes. In the level between Lifetimes we may feel lousy that we blew it and decide we really want to succeed in mastering that important Life lesson. Thus, we may begin this Lifetime with a disease or injury or else get one later so we can better face the previous growth challenge, at which we bet this time we can succeed. And we can - - we do not give ourselves more than we can handle; like learning true self-worth, true personal power, love, determination, courage, emotional honesty, compassion or commitment.

The second way reincarnation influences health involves those of us who choose a disease or injury not out of a growth motive, but out of a limitation. Such a motive that we still carry from another Lifetime might be ignorance, lack of worth, guilt, a desire to punish ourselves, a desire to suffer, Negative Ego, a belief in karma, a despising or disdaining of our body or a belief in domination of illness over health. In these ways our other incarnations influence the choices we make in setting up and living this Lifetime, but they do not determine our events. Indeed, according to metaphysics, once we enter a Lifetime, our power in our present is so focused and so strong and there is so much justice in Life, that if we really want to, we can reverse a decision for disease we made before this Lifetime began. That is how pliable our realities are; nothing is predetermined, not even by us. Thus, the tremendous importance of developing our love, awareness and will in the NOW as we deal with our exploding power to create, like mini-gods, every detail in or not in our TCTCHB Lives.

Most often we have set up our Lifetimes with definite growth foci in mind (once in a while we set up a Lifetime that is just plain ol' Rest and Relaxation). Some of our incarnations have similar emotional issues and that like-energy can resonate with the emotional goals of this one so that our Lifetimes hook-up, as it were, and incarnational influences are exchanged (felt). Jane Roberts, the medium for Seth, referred to these incarnational exchanges as "bleedthroughs". Like everything else in our TCTCHBs, the bleedthroughs we experience are the ones we allow to come through and affect us.

If we become aware of incarnational influences from other Lifetimes that are reinforcing poor health and want to change them, we can work in meditation to help that incarnational self face his issues and succeed. This is the most common reason we let those bleedthroughs occur - - so we can face our unresolved challenges and complete them.

Please remember, when we die we take our emotions with us. They are, in effect, held in "emotional escrow" in our Unconscious Mind. If we acted very cruelly in another Lifetime, for instance, that failure will be stored on the "eliminate-this-shelf" and will likely surface in a Lifetime in which we are more spiritual to give us another chance to change our minds and purify ourselves of that ugliness. Once healed, that incarnational self will stop "broadcasting" cruelty (or heart illness influences) into our current self's reality. Consciously loving self through space and time and identities: how beautiful.

This type of working with our incarnational selves is not necessary to heal our disease conditions; it is a high-class adjunct to our current healing efforts. The biggest reward for doing this type of inner work comes in knowing that we helped another being (actually us then) and that his Life will now be more healed and blessed because of our caring and effort.

So, if reincarnation is of interest to us and we think another Lifetime is resonating with this one and we want to change that influence, then delve into it. If this discussion has been of interest, but is nothing we want to explore, then that is fine, too. What matters the most are the decisions we consciously make now and tomorrow and the next day and the next. Those are the ones that will determine what will happen to us in the weeks ahead. Please remember, in the final analysis, love is what heals.

As far as the body is concerned, reincarnational influences are significantly represented by the creation of birthmarks. Birthmarks can be colored patches of skin, moles, indentations or scars. They are signs we place on our bodies when we are starting this Lifetime to indicate some emotional issue that is important to us. Interpretation of birthmarks follows the same guidelines as interpretation of disease and injury; assess the nature of the mark, the site of the mark, what that site is used for and which chakra is involved.

One researcher I heard about found that through several hypnotic regressions most people with birthmarks recalled a Lifetime, complete with details, in which they had experienced some injury at the site of their current birthmark. It seems they created a mark on their infant body to symbolize the previous wound and the still important emotional issues it symbolizes for them in this Lifetime.

CONCLUSION

From this overview of body systems we can better understand the integrity of the beautiful world we live in. The Great Principle Of Reflectivity allows us to reveal our selves to ourselves through the intelligent dynamics of Body Symbolism.

In the next three chapters we will explore the phenomenon of Body Symbolism in more detail. We will discuss the specific parts of our body and why and how they are used in disease and injury communications. We will also learn the general messages imbued in some common diseases and then we will discuss some important ideas about healing and our beautiful future.

CHAPTER THREE

BODY SPECIFICS

In this chapter we will consider the psychological meanings attached to each external and some internal parts of the body. We will begin this exciting inventory at ground level with our feet and work our way to the top floor of our head.

OUR FEET

Humanity has created living platforms to support us as we move about on Mother Earth.   Feet are our foundations, our grounding. As such, they represent our inner strength and our sense of security.

Some of us greatly tense our foot muscles, creating feet that are knotted upward as if we are ungrounded, afraid to settle down and make full contact with Earth reality. It is as if we are "walking on egg shells", tip-toeing about, afraid of disturbing others' feelings toward us (especially parents and those treated as parents). Some of us train our feet to point in different directions,   with one foot pointing to the left and one to the right, as if we are confused, not sure which way we are going in Life. Oppositionally pointed feet usually indicate a conflict from an early age over self-determination - - whether to walk the path of our true desires and feelings versus walking the route of parental or societal rules. And then some of us train our feet to point inward ("pigeon toed"), as if we feel ashamed of something and are trying to scrunch ourselves inward (often unconsciously trying to hide our genitals). Added to this, inwardly pointing feet ineffectively step on each other, making movement (into sexual maturity) difficult. Others of us create feet with flat arches, as if we seek extra contact with the Earth, extra support. And some of us have feet which are small, frail and non-supportive; pushovers.

Injury or disease to the feet generally indicates a first chakra concern about security. A hurtful foot condition may hinder support or movement, as if we feel unable to stand solidly for ourselves or feel afraid to step forward and be counted. We can also hurt our feet (or other part of our leg) because of feeling insecure about moving into the unknown (a natural fear for Humanity), usually because of fear of handling the responsibility involved in coping. Also, we may be creating and feeling a lot of guilt about some event and injure our feet to stop movement and hold ourselves back from moving into a desired reality. Then again, we may hurt our feet, in effect, to go on a "sit down" strike to either protest unpleasant emotional conditions or get some kindly attention or, scraping the bottom of the emotional barrel, at least some pity. Also, since we naturally express anger through kicking with our feet, we may place a negative condition there because we may want to angrily kick someone, but feel afraid or reluctant to do it, so we symbolically block that desire by injuring our foot instead. Right (masculine) or left (feminine) foot gives a big clue as to with whom we may feel angry.

One of my clients of several years ago was living with her mother, who greatly relied on her for everything. Well, my client was in her 30s and wanted to move out on her own. While we were processing the guilt she felt in doing this, she went ahead with her plans. On the day before she was to move out, she fell off a step and broke her foot. Guess which one? She stayed with her mother until she healed up some and we worked to fully process and release her guilt. Her next departure got off on a good foot and went well.

Toes are a special concern. Humanity has created toes at the anterior ends of our feet because we basically wanted to have a lot of <u>sensual</u> <u>fun</u> with squishy mud, sifting sand and juicy grapes. Besides these noble pleasures, we gave ourselves toes to help us balance while erect. Many of our fellow primates use their toes to secure themselves to trees. Likewise, some of us use our toes to secure ourselves to Earth - - often overcompensating for a fear of falling on our face, thus creating tense, curled toes ("hammer toes"), as if we are continually trying to get a stronger toe-hold on our reality. Disturbances in our toes (especially a chunky experience like gout) indicate we are off balance and insecure in our Life, usually through denial of our emotions.

Less serious foot conditions such as warts, corns, bunions, fungi and calluses indicate insecurity in standing solidly for ourselves. Warts on the soles of our feet, for example, since warts are generally thought of as being "ugly", represent "pockets of ugliness" we feel are inside us, about which we feel insecure, i.e.

makes difficult our stance in or walk forth in Life. This "ugliness" is, of course, emotional and could be inferiority, guilt, rage, vengeance or others. Right or left foot indicates which area of our Life to explore. For instance, I once placed a corn on the little toe of my right foot which I later dissolved through meditation as I took a more secure stance with the expressions of my emotions, particularly with men.

Finally, many of us limit circulation to our feet and experience coldness. Those of us who chronically have "cold feet", however, are those who are withdrawing circulation of energy to our feet because of feeling afraid to take a stand on our issues. In relationships, cold, shivering, knocking feet are mostly related to a fear of a solid, warm stance on the path of commitment.

OUR ANKLES

Moving up, we encounter our beautiful and important ankles. Problems with ankles relate to all the emotional concerns mentioned about feet, especially self-support. Some of us cave our ankles in or out, weakening our body alignment and energy flow. It is as if we did not get enough permission, most often from the same sex parent, to mature and stand up for ourselves.

Ankles, since they are joints, are also concerned with flexibility - - flexibility which allows smooth movement through Life. Also, ankles are created under the influence of the second chakra and represent movement into pleasure. Thus, disturbing our ankles indicates a difficulty with being flexible, moving or supporting ourselves, especially with respect to pleasure. Ankle problems suggest we inspect feelings of fear, anger and guilt.

OUR CALVES, KNEES AND THIGHS

These parts of our body, as a unit, are charged with the first chakra concern of supporting and moving ourselves through physical reality. Knees, however, are second chakra ruled.

Our legs move us further and faster than any other part of our bodies. As such, they represent aggression and long distance planning in our Lives. Some of us feel rather passive and sluggish and may reflect this to ourselves by clumping a lot of fat on our thighs. Bottom-heavy people are working to keep our Life energy down and inhibited. Weak legs indicate a sense of frailty; fear about standing up for ourselves. Whereas, chronically tense, hard legs indicate a heavy compensation for a fear of not being able to support ourselves at all.

Knees, since they are joints, reflect emotional flexibility, especially relating to pleasure. Knees have quite a range of emotional expression: they can knock with fear, bend in submission and defeat, bend pleasurable and aggressively to climb forward and higher or they can extend the lower leg to kick angrily.

We usually give ourselves knee problems to inhibit one or several of these emotional expressions. It is very difficult, for instance, to give someone "a swift kick in the pants" if we have packed our knee full with calcium crystals, one of several conditions we call arthritis. Then there are times we, unfortunately, feel very weak and afraid so, to keep our knees from embarrassingly knocking, we lock our knees with arthritis or injury, symbolizing the stiff-kneed rigidity we think we need to hold ourselves up in the world. And then there are those of us who feel afraid of moving forward into pleasure, so we too lock our knees; as well as those of us who do not want to run, but prefer to limp through Life, often because of fear, guilt, denial of responsibility or seeking pity.

OUR PELVIS

Our pelvis is comprised of our hip bones, our buttocks, our anus and our genitals. It is the outermost of the three cavity-courts of our beloved body temple. Importantly and beautifully, our pelvis, like our head, houses two chakra centers, the first (security) and the second (sensual pleasure).

Most of us in Western culture receive much social conditioning about our pelvises. Classic Paradigm One has never understood the beauty of the pelvis, basically hates it and seeks to deny it into atrophy. Paradigm Two, with the other hand, seeks to exploit the pleasure of the pelvis, viewing it as a storehouse of animalistic urges and wild pleasure to be acted upon mechanically. Most of us have, unfortunately, internalized some of these ideas, so adverse to healthy, pleasurable experience. It is with such self-deprecating notions that we have created the intense fears of feminine energy, love, tenderness and touch so prevalent in our society. Violence, rape, sexual abuse and sexual self-disrespect are the unfortunate, but predictable, manifestations of an unhealthy understanding and experiencing of the marvelous energies resident in our pelvis.

When setting about to create our pelvis (which we do from moment to moment), we consult our emotional experience blueprint. If we have not allowed our sexual urges expression because we feel that we must severely repress them, we may create a small, contracted pelvis. We may also lock our pelvis backwards, as if we are pulling it away from others because frontal contact is threatening. Whereas, if we feel warm, nurturing and perhaps a bit passive, we will likely widen our pelvis. Those of us who feel ashamed of ourselves and/or often masochistically submit to others' demands (either in childhood or now), will tend to tuck our pelvis in, locking it forward like a dog with its tail between its legs. Being so repressed and locked into this "flat ass" posture, we greatly reduce energy and emotion flows through our body.

Our first chakra energy and issue of self-security are housed in our pelvic area. The three areas that symbolize these concerns are our buttocks, our anus and our lower back (coccyx, sacrum and five lumbar vertebrae). Most of us feel insecure at different times of our Lives asking: "Am I good enough? When will I be good enough? How can I try harder? How can I win that approval?" If we create these burdensome weights of insecurity with self, we may reflect these to ourselves with problem conditions in our pelvis.

Buttocks represent our security cushion in the world; they are what we rest upon as we sit. Sometimes, because of shame, fear, guilt, immaturity or laziness, we feel insecure and prefer to passively sit about rather than aggress forth; we then give ourselves large rear cushions to carry around. "Get the lead out of your cushion" is an old expression which speaks to the low energy state symbolized by purposely over-padding our behind. Whereas chronically tense, hard buttocks indicate a "freezing" of muscle, often because of holding back suppressed anger or rage; insecurity and tightening rather than flowing and releasing our "emotional crap".

Hemorrhoids are first chakra manifestations of a bursting insecurity that forces us to "try harder", to squeeze and squeeze out every last bit of effort to maybe please someone out there, often related to our family (blood).

Another first chakra oriented disturbance is becoming very popular - - estimates indicate this unpleasant condition is being selected by half of us in this country. It is the most common reason for us being out of work and on disability leave. Some estimates indicate as much as 121 million work days were lost in 1992 by Americans and 25 billion dollars were spent treating this one condition - - lower back pain.

The lower back is first chakra ruled and that means self-security issues. Lower back problems relate to feeling it a struggle to hold ourselves up, to maintain our balance and not crumble under some oppressive weight. It is as if we are somatically saying: "It's enough to break our back", or feeling like we have no backbone, or feeling "our back is up against the (insecurity) wall."

The major culprit of lower back pain is a perceived lack of self-value and an actual lack of self-love, producing insecurity, often because of the heavy, heavy pressures we place on ourselves by the confusion of our inner worth with our outer worth.

This tragic burden of worth-confusion started for most of us in our childhood when our often similarly-love-starved parents made their approval of us conditional, *i.e.* if we acted the way they wanted, we were "a good boy" or "a good girl"; if we did not behave the way they wanted, we were "a bad boy" or "a bad girl". Thus, in our mind, <u>who</u> we were became confused with <u>how</u> we performed. As we grew up, we continued this toxic confusion of inner and outer worth by internalizing societal definitions which program men to equate their inner worth with their financial prospectus and women to equate their inner worth with their physical attractiveness and/or husband's social position. The big reward of Earthly Life (self-love) is always "out there", dependent on someone's approval, some money, some promotion, some object, some phony power, some whatever; a very false and profoundly, profoundly damaging idea.

Closely associated with this insecurity of self is hurt which comes with the rejection. Lower back pain also can indicate feelings of hurt that have not been felt and released (a weighty burden to carry around).

It is as if we are taught to be a slave to self-rejection. Well, this bale of hurtful insecurity is obviously much too heavy to tote around for very long and our lower back simply hurts and hurts and hurts (as does our heart). Sometimes, after years of stored up misery, we will even ask a vertebral disc to slip out to indicate that we need a rest and cannot "tote that bale" to please our outside approval massa anymore. If we heed our body's call back to ourselves, we can establish self-acceptance as our new massa and liberate ourselves into a true Reconstruction Period that can lead to emotional growth, physical health and joy. Self-acceptance, internal authority and real self-esteem are no burdens; they are lighter than our beautiful, first chakra back bone that supports and balances us.

Moving up the chakras, hipbones form the framework of our pelvis; they carry the weight of the upper body and correspond to second chakra energy. Psychologically speaking, hipbones represent our relationship with pleasure, the pleasure of enjoying our senses. This is wonderful and important symbolism because sensual enjoyment is a much needed, root experience which serves as a foundation, upon which "rests the weight" of further spiritual development, just as the upper body rests upon the pelvis, just as the higher chakras "rest upon" the lower. Also, our hips are joints which represent flexibility in relating to sensuality. Many older people break their hips, perhaps indicating they feel angry about having rigidified their Lives into unpleasurable (and thus unsupportable) routines (ruts). Of course, young people hurt their hips too; delight in our sensual pleasure is a root Human need. When we miss out too much on sensual gratification we are being mean to ourselves; we may reflect this to ourselves in pelvic disturbances.

At this point I would like to clarify what I mean by sensuality or sensual pleasure. Sensuality is a marvelous aspect of Earth Life, which all physical creatures share. Sensuality is the experiencing of Life through our senses. Minerals, since they are made of matter, which is energy and alive, experience awareness through their particular sensing mechanisms. Minerals experience sensual pleasure and will gladly tell you about it, if you care to meditatively listen. In the next complex level of awareness, plants have more developed senses and are thus more capable of sensual pleasure than are minerals. The next level of consciousness, the animal kingdom, has quite a range of complexity and sensuality and can even surpass Humans in the use of some senses. Humans, though, have the highest overall range of sensuality of the four kingdoms of physical Life. Humans not only have outer, physical senses, but also have non-physical, psychic senses, the loving use of which feels very pleasurable. Anyone who wants to, can work diligently to strengthen and refine our mental abilities and perform in a joyous way some of the acts we *currently* call magic. This could include, and is not limited to, knowing the future, conscious telepathy, mentally moving objects around (psychokinesis), teleportation, bi-location, making objects appear or disappear and other such activities.

Not only are Humans the most developed physical species in sensing ability, but we can also experience the highest intensity of pleasure in the use of our senses. We are indeed blessed to be able to think and feel and know the joy of an exciting inspiration or the rapture of purifying beauty. When we stretch our minds we can even net some of the ultra-etheric concepts, which can feel like bursting stars in the core of our senses.

Most of our sensual pleasures, though, are contained in our more "mundane", day-to-day activities. The point is to savor these pleasures, not deny or rush through them like a train speeding through a blurred countryside; slow down, slow down. The intense pleasures of hearing a bird sing or a cat meow or leaves rustle can fill a moment - - our moment - - with tremendous pleasure, if we will but open up and allow it. The sensual joy of feeling smooth fabric or packing our mouth full of squishy pizza, or seeing orange, or touching, really touching skin; the pleasurable, momentary worship of these is what our sensuality is all about.

When we do not allow ourselves our basic Human pleasures, we frustrate our powerful second chakra yearnings. Many of us then go on to more elaborate efforts, sometimes frantic efforts, to kindle a few sparks of pleasure so we can again experience our energy and feel half-way Human. These efforts can range from overeating to hoarding, to obsessive sexual rituals, just to mention a few. And some of us go even further; we have so blocked our pelvic energy and our experience of sensation that we want to be beaten, slapped or whipped, both as part of our emotional masochism and to help loosen our muscular armor so we can finally relax and feel a modicum of second chakra pleasure.

Going slowly, loving in the NOW and attending fully, *gratefully,* to the blessed details of our Lives is a high level prescription for creating the context in which our pleasures can thrive. An important point: enveloping ourselves in increased internal pleasure, we are then more likely to attract even more external pleasure inside our TCTCHBs. When it comes to second chakra energies, please remember that love and pleasure require a leisurely approach. Eight suggested steps: slow down, focus, highlight, feel, enjoy, sigh, be grateful and do it all over again (slowly).

Continuing on with our pelvic inventory, we find (usually at about age two months) located on our pelvis are our genitals, the outer organs of our reproductive system. These are second chakra ruled. Because of the destructive, anti-pleasure messages endemic in our Paradigm One - Paradigm Two society, many of us believe in and create tons of unnecessary guilt about sensual and sexual pleasure. A bacterial, viral or fungal infestation on our genitals generally indicates guilt for experiencing pleasure (mostly because of thinking we are undeserving). These problems can also indicate us wanting more sensual pleasure and feeling angry about not having it. Important to realize: while we may consciously give ourselves permission to indulge, even overindulge, we may unconsciously believe our behavior is "wrong" and worthy of punishment. Such guilt is incredibly destructive and, since it is often unconscious, genital markings are important signals to heed.

In this regard, it is important to note that women receive a very heavy dose of sexual guilt messages as part of our society's institutionalized sexism and pleasure prohibition. There seems to be a huge fear in society about women being freely sexual and somehow becoming lethally promiscuous. This relates to the many cross-cultural myths of "the she devil", the archetype of many men's discomfort (i.e. fear, anger and envy) with female sexuality. This sexual conflict confronts us more now than in the past two thousand years because the birth control pill and other forms of contraception have helped women separate reproduction from sex so they can more freely exercise their personal power and choice.

The primary fear about women being liberated sexually seems to be that our country will somehow "cave in" if we don't keep women at home tending to the family (which is what they are all supposed to want). This fear of female sexuality, diversity and power of expression is a symbol for our fears of feminine energy, creativity and power.

When women explore, actualize and delight in their sexuality, repressed, rigid people who do not do those "sinful" activities, make themselves feel uptight and then slather on guilt-inducing messages. Unfortunately, these messages have been rather effective.

This next idea may sound a bit strange at first, but think about it and you may agree: my friend Lazaris suggests that because many females are oppressed into feeling shamed and uncomfortable about their bodies, their sexuality and their capacity for pleasure, some women and girls allow themselves to get pregnant because of feelings of guilt.

Sounds like this: "If I had such nice, intense sexual pleasure, then I should be punished or else balance out my pleasure-pain ledger and pay a baby-price for it". This guilt choice is tragic because it is totally unnecessary and so easily avoided by simply understanding and accepting that in the wisdom of her choosing to live as a female, she healthfully needs sensual pleasure and enjoys responsible, loving sexual communication. And even if the sex was not responsible or loving, she still does not have to be punished! Wise sexual selections would be nice, indeed very nice, but sometimes we have to bounce ourselves around a bit before we will wake up and honor our Child Within. But guilt and punishment? Preferably not.

And this common, guilt-oriented belief about having to balance out a pleasure with a pain can only sabotage our evolutionary fun. This ledger-sheet approach to sensual pleasure is based on several ideas and here are two of the main ones: one, a guilt for receiving too much pleasure because of a belief in scarcity ("There is not enough pleasure - - abundance - - to go around so I cannot always have pleasure and take it away from someone else, so I will expect - - attract - - some pain now. Aren't I good?"). Secondly, many of us believe we are not deserving and have to <u>earn</u> the right to feel pleasure, but have not yet done so (probably never will). So when we do give ourselves some pleasure, we think we have to attach some pain to it because we have not yet earned the right to have it at all. Of course, the truth of the cosmos is there is no undeserving, no guilt, no ledger-sheet, no need to "pay the price" and no need to earn any pleasure. But, if we believe these tragically anhedonic ideas, we will attract the corresponding unpleasant events and live them out as our physical reality. A more accurate picture is that, in our private TCTCHBs, love and abundance are happily, sloppily available to anyone and everyone who is consciously and unconsciously willing to experience them. And that is our Lifetimes' challenge: to understand this abundance and attain the willingness to allow it for ourselves (if that fits into our plan of spiritual development).

Another emotion motivating genital disturbance is fear, especially fear of receiving love (true sexual pleasure being a high expression of giving and receiving love). This is a very important and lengthy topic, one which Lazaris has contributed much to our understanding. Basically, fear of receiving love is learned in childhood because of the "strings" often attached to love and because of common negative beliefs about self-worth, suffering, how to "earn" love and how much love (success) one can have. Genital markings of herpes and warts may flare up at times when we are feeling especially afraid or feeling undeserving to receive love (not only in a sexual way, but in a general, pleasurable way, too).

In summary, sensual pleasure is a <u>need</u> we all have. In our Paradigm Two, TECHNE-lopsided, time-rushed society with its attendant Paradigm One, "sin-devil-evil-guilt" pleasure prohibitions, sensual pleasure is the Sirens' call, harkening us home - - home to love of our spirituality, our Humanity, our selves and our beloved bodies.

OUR ABDOMEN

Our abdomen is our body section that houses our third chakra energies and our organs of digestion and absorption. Our belly is in the front and our back is in back. Let us discuss our stomach area first.

Our belly is the most tender, vulnerable part of our body; we have bones above and bones below, but no hard structures to protect our guts. Humans have chosen, you see, to relatively expose our guts to highlight to ourselves the importance emotional vulnerability (i.e., honesty) plays in our evolution. Our stomach area is a powerful energy center in which food is transformed into the components to nourish our physical Life, which are then distributed to our cells. In a similar fashion and one step inward, emotional energy is processed in our third chakra stomach area and distributed throughout our system to nourish our spiritual Life.

Those of us who process emotions well usually do not locate difficulties in our belly region (nor other areas of our body, unless we want to). Those of us, however, who "can't stomach" our reality or feelings or who feel our (repressed) emotions are "eating us up" are likely to symbolize these experiences to ourselves in our abdomen. Apparently we feel that way a lot in our society, as reflected by the fact that one of the largest selling prescription drugs in America, Tagamet, is an anti-ulcer medication. When we repress and stagnate our emotions, we commonly communicate our imbalance via stomach or intestinal upsets. What it seems to come down to is this: those who have the guts to spill their guts are those who will well maintain their guts.

OUR THORAX

Our thorax, or chest area, is the second court of our body temple. In this court burn the two fires of respiration and circulation. Our thorax is comprised of a sternum, twelve ribs, twelve costal cartilages (which connect our ribs to our sternum) and twelve thoracic vertebrae.

There are four basic styles of thorax construction. The first style we can call balanced - - a chest that is normally shaped and proportioned and one that moves easily with each breath.

Secondly, there is the overexpanded type. This is a defensive, rigid style of keeping ourselves "puffed up", chosen by those who think we will somehow protect ourselves by not completely exhaling. It seems we fear what would happen if we fully let go; we fear softening and being vulnerable; we fear feeling again.

When we grow up feeling insecure and ungrounded, we may reflect this to ourselves by creating weak, thin legs. As we get older, we may build a massive upper structure to compensate for our hurt, weak feelings and non supportive legs. Unfortunately, this defense does not work the way we hoped it would. As mentioned in the section on "character armor", an expanded, rigid, thoracic shell helps decrease sensitivity and emotional experience, which goes to further diminish our security stance (legs). Feeling insecure and losing emotional sensitivity and meaning, many people then overcompensate by exaggerating ego importance and ego goals such as status, appearance, money and material possessions. Because we have diminished our range of feeling and intuition to keep our chest "puffed up", we tend to not feel satisfied in our bodies and easily become out of touch with what is real and has meaning for us. The expanded chest type makes for the worst of politicians; those who only think and do not feel, the ideologue who would unleash a war as a matter of some abstract, egoically clutched principle.

The third style of chest construction is the asymmetrical chest, one which has a different sized or shaped right half from the left half, or a different upper half from the lower half. A person with an asymmetrical chest is experiencing a twist of body which reflects twists in emotion, especially conflicts over love (very similar to what occurs in the condition of scoliosis). An example of this construction: a child who is caught in the middle of warring parents who becomes conflicted about which parent is ok to love or love more.

The fourth style of chest creation is the sunken or hollow look. If we collapse our chest we restrict our breathing and lower our energy and emotion flows. It is as if we are trying to push our chest and heart in, to recede them away from threatening contact with the world as a defense against further hurt. A hollow in our chest represents a kick to the heart, usually received when young, delivered by one or both parents. The hollow can also indicate heart-felt issues which we carry over from another Lifetime.

Psychologically speaking, the front of our thorax, our chest, represents pride ("Stick your chest out"). It is a fourth chakra governed area. The rear of our thorax is our mid-back, rising to the base of our neck. Difficulties in this section of our back indicate feelings of strain and anger at emotional burdens (especially guilt) that we are carrying.

Problems in our chest area usually indicate difficulties around love. In the common, painful condition of heartburn (now called acid reflux), for instance, hydrochloric acid backs up the esophagus past the pyloric valve, causing a burning sensation in the heart area. This condition indicates that "acidic feelings" are backing up in our system, from the third chakra to the fourth. This indicates that, usually through repeated frustrations and angers, we think-feel that it hurts to love.

The common conditions of a heart attack, narrowing of cardiac arteries and other heart problems usually indicate feelings of a "broken heart" (i.e. disappointment, sadness, anger) about giving or receiving love with self and/or others. Sometimes, however, we will live in a world of love that is just fine, but will choose a heart "attack" as an expedient and rather tidy way of ending our Lifetime. Again, our motives are highly individualized and must be interpreted that way.

BREASTS

In this discussion we will focus on the breast area of the Human female. Breasts are fleshy, fatty extensions of the chest wall. The major function of a female's breasts is to house milk producing glands which a mother uses to nourish her infant (if she chooses to have one). Each breast has four such glands and a nipple opening.

Lately in American society, women's breasts have been made into objects. Manipulations of fashion have alternately sought to minimize breasts (as in the '20s) and expand breasts (in the '50s and '60s). In the '80s, fashion and bionics gave us implanted breasts and all the problems attached therewith. The importance placed on women's breasts as a fashion accessory seems to be approaching the dimensions of a cultural fetish. Many men and women are being programmed to equate a woman's worth (confused with her sex appeal) with her mammary stature (basketball sized breasts - - what's with that?). We are losing awareness of the bio-importance of breasts, as sites of a nourishing, loving exchange. We are making breasts into objects of fashion, objects of conquest and, ultimately, objects of mutual rejection.

Psychologically speaking, breasts can represent several emotional experiences. Because breasts are a characteristic of the female sex and because of the undue, egoic importance our culture places on them, breasts often represent a woman's sense of identity.

Thus, when women internalize negative beliefs about being a woman, requisition negative experiences and then get (justifiably) angry about the programming and treatment received, they may symbolize their anger in their breasts. Since they feel unloved, the fourth chakra chest area is involved. Some women have been emotionally abused and feel so angry about it that they, as difficult as this may be to accept, actually prefer to remove their "incriminating" organs altogether. Thus, cancer and mastectomies may be chosen. Or, these women may feel angry about not being allowed to love, not being allowed to nourish and be nourished. If a woman creates a disturbance, particularly cancer, in her left breast, this usually indicates anger about non-acceptance of her own feminine energy (particularly her emotions, imagination and creativity). The negative condition could also indicate anger about being mistreated as a woman and/or anger at her mother, mothering figures or other women for the limitations taught her about being a female. A disturbance, particularly cysts, tumors or cancer, located in her right breast usually indicates anger about either a non-acceptance of her masculine energy, particularly her intellect and the practical implementation of her truth. It could also indicate an anger about a non-nurturing, over-reliance on her masculine energy to get along. The negative condition could also indicate anger at the men in her Life - - father, husband(s), brother(s) and /or male oriented society (particularly with our institutionalized sexist standards and treatment).

Many men, especially the more sensitive of us, may want to know why some women feel so angry about their womanhood. The obvious answer is they do not feel angry about their womanhood itself, but they feel angry about the profound oppression, cruelty and punishment heaped on their womanhood throughout history. With this heavy sexual oppression usually comes concomitant feelings of inferiority, powerlessness, shame, hopelessness, rage and depression. These hurtful emotions can easily muck up our internal peace and, with repetitive repressions, can then mightily distort our external body.

Equality in all aspects of emotional and societal Life (esteem, sex, race, sexual orientation, economics and politics) is the only antidote to the poison of hurting each other. Again, this most certainly involves balancing our masculine energy dominated society with sweet infusions of mystic, feminine energy.

There are two basic reasons why it is vitally important that men realize that to further oppress women is to oppress ourselves. First, the hurts we do to others always hurt ourselves. Hurting others always lowers true self-esteem and always messes up our emotional Life, thus retarding our spiritual development. Also, when men hurt women, we, of course, make unsafe and so sad our society and global village.

Secondly, it would be wise and helpful for everyone to realize that men and women are connected to each other and, in Lifetimes concurrent, actually are each other. We experience each sex as a necessary means of spiritual growth. In other Lifetimes, current men are then women and then men are current women (similarly, in other Lifetimes we are *all* races and sexual orientations - - a most important and beautiful realization, eh, racists and gay bashers?). Harmful attitudes toward The Other always, always work against self, because The Other is self. Sexism and other forms of bigotry are spiritual poison and therefore ugly. Sexism permeates everything in our world and is not to be underestimated in its lethal effects on our own and society's heart and development. We would do very well to work in a deliberate, conscious way to remove sexism from our psychic fabrics. The sooner we become equals with each other and then friends and then brothers and sisters, the better.

OUR SHOULDERS

Our shoulders are ball and socket joints which allow us to reach forward, backward and around. We need free use of our shoulders to fully use our arms and hands. Thus, shoulders are particularly involved with aggression and are associated with work ("Put your shoulder to the wheel") and social responsibility ("should-ers").

The basic types of shoulder construction are these: balanced, weak, overly developed and overly rounded. Also, we can hold our shoulders in balanced, upward, forward or retracted positions. Frail shoulders indicate feelings of weakness and inability to aggressively reach out for nourishment or desired events. Overly developed shoulders can indicate an exaggerated sense of responsibility ("big shoulders" to lean on) and/or overcompensating strength. Overly rounded, slumped shoulders indicate feeling emotionally burdened and overwhelmed. Shoulders that are locked upward and forward indicate fear, shame or guilt; a wanting to withdraw into our chest like a turtle. Shoulders that are locked forward assist in creating a collapse or hollow in the chest area; this indicates a desire to shield and protect our heart from expected hurt. Shoulders that are locked backward, held in check "military style" indicate anger with a readiness to fight or a fear of reaching out or both. Shoulders that are well proportioned and held in a relaxed, balanced way indicate an expectation to be able to safely reach out and get what we like.

As stated, shoulders relate to carrying emotional burdens and responsibility. Being situated so close to the throat area, shoulders are created and maintained under the influence of fifth chakra energies. This follows from the central spiritual truth that our primary "load to carry" in these Lifetimes is our responsibility for full, honest expression of our emotions. Thus, when we create difficulties in our shoulders we are symbolizing being tired of carrying some burden, usually resulting from a lack of self-expression, such as not communicating anger, hurt, guilt or fear, not asking for help, not asserting our rights or not giving compliments.

Of the emotions we repress and burden ourselves with, few are as pernicious as guilt, a feeling that is <u>not</u> a part of true Human nature, but one that has been societally taught and is totally unnecessary. Guilt is anger that a person thinks is wrong to express, so that the anger is turned back on ourselves as a negative judgment. As an example, let's say I am driving along and a goose walks in front of my car and I can't stop in time from hitting him and injuring him. I then think: "Oh, I'm so dumb! No, wait a minute. That damn goose walked in front of my car. It's his fault! Why did he have to pick my car to waddle in front of? Why didn't he at least honk? No, wait. I can't think that. It was a poor, dumb goose. It didn't know any better. That's wrong to think (and feel) that anger. Actually, I just feel guilty for hitting the poor goose." Allowing ourselves to recognize and process out our anger is the crucial step in releasing guilt. Then we hopefully would assess the reasons why we allowed the goose to pick our car, i.e., what it means to us.

Guilt is used as a tool to dominate ourselves and/or others and is also used as a hefty means of punishment. A difficulty in the front part of our shoulder relates to oneself; the back of our shoulder to others.

OUR UPPER ARMS

Arms are our major tools for manipulating our physical environment. Upper arms, like our thighs, relate to muscle capacity; they are the power house of arm function. The circulatory flow of Life energy is such that it enters our left, feminine side and exits our right, masculine side. This flow is symbolized in our arms; our left, feminine arm symbolizes receiving nourishment and pleasure from the world and our right, masculine arm symbolizes giving out our feelings and talents to the world.

People who create thin, frail arms indicate blocked aggression and a withdrawal of energy. Low vitality arms indicate feelings of weakness in taking in what one wants and/or weakness in keeping out what one does not want. A person with overdeveloped arms may be compensating for a fear of being weak or indicating a conflict between wanting to reach out and holding back at the same time. Upper arms weighted with fat indicate a sluggishness in aggression.

Disease or injury constructions placed in the upper arms usually relate to feelings of anger, fear or guilt about giving out (right arm) and anger, fear or guilt about receiving love (left arm). Dominant arm problems may also represent anger, even an unexpressed desire to strike out and hit someone (not recommended).

OUR ELBOWS AND FOREARMS

Our elbows are hinge joints that are created by third chakra energy. Elbows represent flexibility and house the part of our body that has the most mystical name of any body part - - our funny bone.

Difficulties located in our elbows generally represent an accumulation of third chakra, contracting emotion (anger, fear, sadness), leading to inflexibility in receiving (left) or giving (right). Problems in the left elbow can also indicate anger at a woman/women for not receiving from her/them the pleasure and caring we want or anger at not being allowed to give to her/them as we want. Problems in our right elbow can indicate anger at a man/men for not receiving from him/them the pleasure and caring we want or anger at not being allowed to give to him/them as we want.

Our forearms are similar in psychology to our upper arms. Our lower arm and its energy is less massive, more refined and symbolizes competence in detailed work. Lower arm difficulties also represent issues of giving (right arm), taking (dominant arm), receiving (left arm) and hitting (dominant arm).

OUR WRISTS

Our wrists are ellipsoid joints which are governed by second chakra energies. Wrists, therefore, represent sensual pleasure. We may injure or place a disease condition in our left wrist if we feel inferior, afraid or guilty about receiving pleasure or love or if we feel angry at a woman/women for not letting us receive more pleasure or love. We may injure or disease our right wrist if we feel inferior, afraid or guilty about giving pleasure or love or if we feel angry about giving any more pleasure or love, especially to a man/men or to the world.

OUR HANDS

Our hands are bony, flesh covered projections, the most refined part of our arm system. Hands take, give, seize, strike, hold, caress and manipulate. We create large, small, strong, frail, thin and fat hands. Each style makes a statement about our inner relationship to aggression.

Hands are the body tool we use to do delicate, detailed work. A particularly important relationship exists between our thumb and index finger, a cooperative venture that allows detailed focusing of our minds through our hands so we can successfully manipulate matter to a highly specific degree. Thumb-forefinger cooperation and coordination is an Earthly evolutionary mechanism whereby Humanity builds our tools, writes our ideas and gently, lovingly squeezes another's body parts to give pleasure. The opposite polarity is there, too, in that we use this part of our hand to arrange and activate the knives, guns, bombs and missiles of our world.

Health problems in our right hand deal with emotional issues about giving of self. "Am I good enough to give?", "Am I powerful enough to give?", "Is what I give of value?", or: "Hell no, I am too damn mad to give anything!".

Injury or disease to our right hand can also symbolize issues of anger and sadness with men in our Lives. On the other hand, health difficulties on our left side deal with issues about receiving: "Damn, I never get what I want!", "No, I do not deserve to receive", "I am afraid to receive" or: "It's too late! I am not going to receive it, even though I really, really want it. Screw you!" Disease or injury of the left hand can also symbolize issues of anger and sadness with women in our Lives.

There is a distinction between internal and external hand problems. Internal difficulties relate to muscle (sense of power), bone (sense of security), blood (family) or nerves (awareness). External problems (skin) relate to our image of ourselves as a giving (right) or receiving (left) person.

Disease or injury to our fingers usually indicates anger or fear of being detailed in our Lives ("detailed" in spiritual terms translates into being truthful, especially about our beliefs and feelings). Our third finger has to do with love - - injury here often indicates anger at not being loved enough. It is interesting that our culture intuitively singled out this finger for the wearing of rings symbolizing love and marital commitment. I imagine you can guess which emotion is indicated by an injury to our second finger.

OUR NECK

Our neck is a bony, muscular, visceral channel which very importantly and most admirably connects our head to our body. Our neck contains our throat (pharynx), which delivers food and air to their home organs. Out neck also contains our epiglottis and larynx. The epiglottis is our oral traffic controller, directing food down our esophagus, keeping it away from our larynx. Our larynx, of course, is our "voice box", a cartilaginous bulb which contains ligaments that vibrate at various frequencies when we push air past them. These are our vocal cords, our main organs of speech. Fifth chakra energies reside here and govern our neck area.

In styles of neck creation, we have the basic three: balanced, long and short. A long neck indicates a desire to avoid our feelings, to elevate our awareness (head) far above our heart and guts so as to retreat to the "safety" of intellectualization.

Long necks may also indicate a personality who is a dreamer, one who dwells in imagination and whose head is "stuck in the clouds." Short necks indicate a desire to hide, to retreat turtle-like into our thorax. This indicates childhood feelings of shame and fear, usually from violent punishments, so that we want to protect ourselves and not do anything to "stick our necks out." We may also want to avoid the responsibility of action, which comes with awareness or we may be avoiding imagination, preferring to live as a rather Earth-bound personality.

Psychologically speaking, problems with our neck may indicate several motives, each having to do with awareness and expression of self. Our neck is a pivotal joint; we use it to turn this way and that, to look this way and that. If we do not want to be flexible and look at new ideas or face some realization about ourselves or others, we may symbolize this reluctance by creating a stiff neck so that we can comfortably look in one (avoidant) direction only. Also, because we use our necks to hold our heads high with pride, we may hurt our neck to symbolize that we believe and feel we cannot honestly hold our head with pride. If we are very rigid in our self-definitions or are fearfully avoiding self- inspection, we may reflect these with the more serious, locking condition of arthritis.

Sometimes we hold back our expression of anger at someone and instead give ourselves "a pain in the neck", as we feel that person to be. Sore throats generally indicate difficulty (soreness) in expressing self, often because of fear or guilt; feeling we would make too many waves, be "bad", be rejected or get into trouble. Sore throats may also be an angry closing off of communication. Laryngitis generally indicates a more intense fear, guilt or anger about expression. A more severe condition like a muscular constriction of our throat may indicate feelings of anger and not wanting to have opinions or obligations "shoved down our throat" anymore or finding some situation "hard to swallow" (even success). Increasing in intensity, a cancer condition in the neck indicates raging anger and withheld expression of it. Cancer of the esophagus indicates anger at others and ourselves for having swallowed our experiences and others' lies, expectations and opinions without expression of our true feelings. Tumors of the trachea indicate so much anger not expressed that it becomes smothering, actually choking off our air supply. Again, motive analysis depends on our unique, individualized emotional world. If we sing or talk for a living, for instance, we may give ourselves problems with our larynx because we do not want to sing or talk for a living anymore, or because we want to "punish" people by withholding our expression or punish ourselves by attacking our source of livelihood. We could also be communicating a message to ourselves that our Negative Ego is over-running our communication and that we had better get it under control or stunt our growth or even that we are afraid of that happening.

OUR HEAD

Our head is our skull, a bony chamber covered on the outside with fine accouterments of flesh and hair. Our head is designed to house four of our five major physical senses: sight, hearing, smell and taste. Our skull is comprised of a collection of flat and angular bones that fit together like a jig saw puzzle, except for our jaw which happens to be fastened at a joint. Most importantly, our head is the third, innermost court of our sacred body temple, represented as the Holy of Holies. In it resides our beautiful brain, the magnificent physical counterpart of our non-physical consciousness.

Our head has two sides, front and back. We will discuss the back, then the front. Injury or disease to the back of our head usually represents some issue we are unaware of "hitting us from behind." This is often symbolic of repressed emotion, often centered around fear. If we, for instance, fear our emotions because we believe the common superstition that they will make us dangerously unstable and we prefer instead to try to think them away, we may attract a blow to the back of our (thinking) head to symbolize our fear of being similarly zapped by our "nasty" feelings or to symbolize that we ought to stop over-thinking so much. Or, if we happen to believe this is a horrible world we live in and we cannot safely turn our back on our neighbor, then we may attract a blow to the back of our head to symbolize such negative beliefs, especially at the site where we hold those beliefs.

OUR FACE

The front of our head is our face. It is comprised of several structures (jaw, lips, nose, cheeks, eyes) and we will discuss them from the bottom up.

We usually show our emotional Life most clearly through our face. Our face, similar to our skin, represents our persona, the image we present to the world. Usually we have an array of emotions that are revealed thorough our faces. Some of us, however, have sculpted and hardened certain expressions into our faces, making them rather mask-like (expressions such as surprised, fearful, suspicious, angry and others). These facial masks may indicate our repetitive emotional experience or they may be worn as a devious cover-up for our true feelings and motivations.

In a less severe way, it is fairly common to create our face with two or three different groups of features. For instance, many people create the left-feminine side of our face differently from our right-masculine side. And some of us create the top half of our face differently from the bottom half (as you look into a mirror, cover the left half of your face with a piece of paper, then the right; then the top, then the bottom. Notice any differences?). These facial "splits" indicate conflicts in our emotional Life, usually between our masculine and feminine energies and/or relationships with our fathers and mothers.

Another facial characteristic to be aware of is immobility. As mentioned, some of us arrange our faces into rigid expressions. And some of us go further and immobilize portions of our face or even our whole face. When we do this we are trying to numb and hide our emotional expression - - likely believing (most often from childhood) that it is unsafe for us to "face" our own feelings or to show our feelings, usually because of harsh or violent punishments.

Psychologically speaking, our face represents how we "face" our selves and the world; disease or injury to our face indicates a problem concerning our self-image.

With a hurt or disfigured face we make it more difficult to "put our best face forward" because we have, in a sense, "lost face" with ourselves. We may create an unappealing condition (a rash on our face is a good example) because we have a difficult time facing the truth about ourselves because it conflicts with our self-image. It is important to understand the feared truth may not be all that terrible (and usually is not), but we may judge it to be and then fight and hurt ourselves emotionally. Or, we may create an unappealing facial countenance because in another Lifetime we relied too much on facial beauty and did not develop a loving relationship with our soul and we do not want to take that chance again.

This is a good place to explore that last point further. In our objectifying, advertising, consumerist culture we very highly value a pretty face, especially for women. Pretty faces of women are used to sell almost all products, from booze to cars, to television, to soap and many others. In balance this, like most anything else, is ok, but our culture has gone nuts over pretty faces. Unfortunately, many good people buy into our culture's superstition about media beauty, compare ourselves, find ourselves lacking and painfully get down on ourselves as being of little value. This is very sad because love and wisdom and fun and the growth of our soul and Higher Self care nothing about facial features.

An important point to realize about having a pretty face or not is that the facial features we wear, like all else in our TCTCHB, are chosen. Sometimes a child knows or just thinks his mom and/or dad will not love him if he does not have a pretty face. So, he will choose an appealing facial structure. But for him, physical attractiveness is a symbol of his pain at the perceived conditional acceptance from his parents.

As for our cultural superstition that someone with a pretty face is better than someone who has a "plain" face : HA ! First of all, how in the world can one person be "better than" another? Secondly, how can one who chose physical attractiveness be better than one who chose something different? Also to consider, of course, is the fact that judging what is pretty is relative to the current definitions of the culture; it is a completely arbitrary value unfortunately applied in an absolutist fashion.

In this regard, it is time we "face" the truth: a pretty face is a choice no better than or worse than any other choice, just different. "The Elephant Man" had an inner light that burned brighter than some "pretty" people could ever guess possible.

With respect to disease or injury, there are seven reasons I am aware of why someone would choose a damaged countenance.

A facial disturbance may be created because we may consciously or unconsciously appear ugly to ourselves and thus wish to appear ugly to others. We may also choose a facial disturbance because of feelings of guilt and/or shame, a desire to punish ourselves, a desire to get pity, a desire to win approval by being one-down or the same as someone we want to win over (often a parent or sibling), or as a way to push people away because of fear or anger. Also, as an unappealing countenance could be chosen to guard against us playing destructive ego games we think we would play if we had a handsome countenance. A disturbance on the left side of our face indicates a self-image issue with our feminine energy or females; disruptions on the right side of our face indicate self-image issues with our masculine energy or males.

Acne is a common disruption of facial calm, usually created in the adolescent stage of our Lifetime. Acne seems to have three basic emotional meanings. First, it is indicative of angry feelings that are erupting in puss-filled mounds of tension. In adolescence, many of us want to separate from our family and be more independent, but are usually restricted from doing so. The tension within us, especially if our parents tend toward smothering, can erupt facially. It is as if our self-image of increasing independence conflicts too much with the imposed dependence of cultural and family structures. The second emotional meaning of acne relates to a conflict some adolescents may feel about familial separation - - wanting to leave and yet not wanting to; the conflict of separation can explode in their image of themselves: Who am I, a kid or an adult? The internal tension over which face to present to the world can erupt as a blemished, conflicted face. The third emotional motive for acne is the aforementioned desires to mar our appearance.

It is interesting to note that not only do we choose an attractive or plain face, but before birth we manipulate our genes to style our faces to resemble the face of the parent or sibling(s) we feel close to or want to feel close to. We will discuss these dynamics more in the section on heredity in the next chapter.

OUR JAW

Our jaw is a hinge joint we use for two important processes, eating and talking. Our jaw is symbolic of aggression - - to assert our right to eat, our right to nourishment, and our right to express ourselves. We create small jaws, medium jaws and large jaws; we hold our jaws in balanced, extended or retracted positions. An extended jaw indicates a lot of determination, but if frozen in this position, it can indicate a defense against softening and crying. A retracted jaw indicates less assertiveness and more timidity. A freezing of our jaw in the retracted position may indicate a crying response that is just waiting to happen.

Our jaw also serves as the brain's censor - - clamping down on disallowed expressions (most often anger) through prolonged contractions of muscles. This often leads to grinding our teeth while awake and especially while asleep. Instead of grinding our words into silence or grunts, it would be much more healthful to "chew" someone else out (with harm to none). According to Bioenergetics, tension in our jaw usually correlates with tension in our pelvis. Also, a muscle block in our jaw hinders the flow of energy to our eyes.

Our jaw involves our chin, a part of us which often indicates emotional blows received. As an example, when my very good friend was in great health trouble, her closest female friend and I both manifested huge blemishes on the left sides of our chins at the same time; it is as if the bad news came from a female (left side) and both of us "took it on the chin."

OUR NOSE

Our proboscis is a triangularly shaped mound of fibrocartilage which protrudes from our face. It serves the very fine functions of purifying and warming the air we breathe and serving as a locus for our sense of smell. Closely situated to our nasal cavities are four groups of smaller cavities called sinuses. These hollows in our skull serve two important functions; one, they lighten our skull so that it is easier to transport around (face it; we are all airheads !) and two, sinuses add timbre to our voice. Our voices change - - become deeper, less distinct when these epithelial lined cavities become filled with mucous, often through a "told in da noze."

Psychologically speaking, our nose relates to our respiratory system, our worldly appearance and our pleasure of smell. Let us inspect each area.

Difficulties in breathing relate to the concerns mentioned earlier about backlogged emotions and feeling suffocated. Difficulties in breathing through our nose usually occur in the "common" cold, allergies and sinus blockages (discussed in Chapter Four).

Next, our nose is obviously an important aspect of our facial appearance. We give ourselves straight, crooked, hooked, narrow, pug, upturned, broad noses, etc. Disease, injury or blemishes placed on our outer nose may indicate a desire to mar our facial image because of insecurity, guilt or self-punishment. We may also be giving ourselves a message not to "stick our nose where it does not belong" or to get in better control of our Negative Egos so we do not "look down our nose" at others.

Damage to our sense of smell indicates a desire to reduce our pleasure, usually because something about us or others "smells bad" to us, usually because of guilt, self-hate and/or fear. To the degree we communicate with each other by smell, our nose is also affected by fifth chakra energies.

OUR LIPS

Our lips are fifth chakra influenced fleshy folds use primarily for communication through talking and kissing. Injury or disease to our lips generally indicates a conflict over expressing ourselves. Also, because lips are an important sexual organ (second chakra pleasure), lip disturbances may relate to conflicts about giving love/pleasure, receiving love/pleasure or self-image.

Cold sores and fever blisters result when a virus (Herpes) is allowed to bloom. We allow this to happen because we want to draw attention to our lips and our relationship to self-expression. A sore on our lip can indicate at least two experiences: one, a feeling of having to "bite our lip" to get along. The tension from our quelled expression - - often felt as an emotional blistering - - becomes manifest as a physical blistering. From my own experience, I always know when I have betrayed myself through repressing my true expression because I give myself one of those damn sores. I then express my "soreness" at myself, apologize, work through the disowned expression, forgive myself and affirm all the more that I will more honestly express my feelings, at least to myself, starting now.

Lip sores can also symbolize feelings of guilt or self-punishment because we have said something we wish we had not. Lip sores can be reminders that we would be better off next time to "bite our lip", especially when we have made the serious error of hurting someone through our verbal expression.

OUR TONGUE

Our tongue is a muscular organ lined with mucosa. Our tongue was our original antenna when we were infants - - we licked the table leg, the dog, the mommy, the car and everything else. We did this because our tongue is the most sensitive body apparatus at that stage of our development. With a sense of security achieved through the satisfying use of our tongue, hopefully, we went forward in Life and discovered other sources of security and pleasure such as sound, smell, touch and later self and abstract meanings. In this regard, our tongue is influenced by first chakra energies. Unfortunately, some of us keep ourselves rather stuck in our oral experience. Not quite making the transition to other forms of self-security, we still rely heavily on our tongue and mouth. We may express our security needs through heavy eating or smoking, sometimes building the dependence and behavioral patterns into addictions.

Our tongue also operates under the influence of second chakra energies. Our tongue contains many chemical receptors known as taste buds, which send impulses to our brain which are then interpreted as pleasurably or unpleasurably salty, bitter, sour or sweet. Finally, our tongue is a key organ of speech and thus relates to fifth chakra energies.

Disease or injury to our tongue may relate to first, second or fifth chakra issues or all of them. We may damage our tongue to communicate the same message as with a cold sore ("bite your tongue"). We may also hurt our tongue to indicate guilt or anger about what we spoke or did not speak in the recent past or even as a psychic message to ourselves to hinder what we might be tempted to speak in the future. Finally, we may damage our tongue to hinder our sensual pleasure of taste.

OUR TEETH

Our teeth are bone-like projections which grow out of our skull. Our teeth contain enamel, the hardest substance in our body. Teeth are of great importance in the fine functions of eating, talking and smiling.

Disease or injury to our teeth indicate emotional concerns related to one or all of the above functions. We may harm our teeth to indicate security concerns about assertiveness, perhaps feeling we are being blocked in doing what we want to do, so we cannot really "sink our teeth" into our reality and "chew on" the meanings of our Lifetime.

Teeth are also indicative of emotional concerns about self-expression. Since teeth are made of bone-like material, they indicate a structure for security. Thus, hurt teeth may indicate an insecurity about what we are expressing, such as: is what we say true? Is our truth good enough? Also, tooth issues could indicate a desire to express intense anger through biting words and tearing into someone; or a fear of doing same, so as to break a tooth as a symbolic, preventive measure.

Finally, teeth are related to the image we present to the world. Is our image-smile clean and bright or darkened with film (doubt and fear)?

OUR SPEECH

I want to make special mention of a very important point. It is with our just discussed larynx, lips, tongue and teeth that we express ourselves verbally. Words are incredibly important to Humanity as a tool of communication, thus the placement of our speech organs "higher up" the chakra scale, close to our spiritual centers.

It is through the wise, loving use of our fifth chakra organs of speech that we help ourselves elevate our consciousness as we open our hearts. We, in effect, channel our first, second, third and fourth chakra concerns up and out of our fifth chakra capabilities. Our energy is rising up our spinal rivers, out our mouths on the way to our seventh chakra and beyond, home to our Higher Selves.

Here is the central issue for us: is what we are expressing verbally of high enough quality to send back to our Higher Selves through our interactions with others? Pretty heavy concept: what we say to others in our daily interactions is absorbed by our Higher Selves and helps create them as they create us. Thus, how we express ourselves verbally is a very important area of our Lives to inspect, evaluate and, if not loving enough, change. As we hurt others through low quality verbal expressions, we diminish ourselves and our Higher Selves! Our evolution is our preferred future and hopefully we will realize we must carefully tend to how we daily use our important organs of speech to enhance, uplift and bless ourselves and others.

Indeed, The New Age is the enhanced use of speech as well as thought and action. "Enhanced", of course, means more loving; all that is important, all that is spiritual, all that is beautiful is loving. As Humanity focuses on the wise and kind use of our speech center, we will more successfully negotiate bridges of understanding to cooperatively rebuild our relationships, society and world village.

OUR CHEEKS

Disease, blemishes or injury affecting our facial cheeks can be a symbolic "slap on the cheek", indicating self-reproach, guilt or shame. Similarly, but less intense, blushing is a rush of blood to our cheeks which indicates embarrassment about an idea.

OUR EYES

Our eyes are marvelous organs of creation; we create a whole world with them. Each eye is an extension of nervous tissue from our brain. Our eyes are sense organs that read our environment and are dependent upon light. Indeed, one may say that light allowed our eyes to develop, for without light, a person begins to atrophy their eyes. Many child laborers, for instance, who worked the coal mines of Pennsylvania and Kentucky in the early 20th century, gradually went blind because, on the physical level, they did not use their eyes for perceiving a strong enough light.

It has been often said "The eyes are the windows to the soul" and indeed they are. Our eyes reflect most clearly our emotional experience and indicate the quality of our Life energy. Thus, some of us create our eyes to look sad, dreamy, cold, sparkling, frenzied, glazed or intense. Sometimes we will withdraw our energy from our eyes and wear a mask with a dull, vacant look.

It is as if we do not want anyone looking into the windows of our soul or emotional system; we do not want any energy coming out of our eyes because of some perceived threat, usually fear of what would happen if we expressed our feelings, usually our anger, i.e., "shot daggers" out of our eyes.

An exciting field of study, iridology, suggests all important emotional experiences are recorded in our iris, the pigmented circular rim around the pupil. Iridologists say they can "read" the variations in our iris and discern emotional relationships of the past, the future and can also assess current organ malfunctions. Indeed, this makes logical sense because of the holographic nature of Earth Life, in which every part of the whole contains the whole. I am sure iridology is a field of inquiry that will soon open up to the "light" of day and finally be "seen" for what it is. The above quotes indicate the psychospiritual functions of our eyes; to open up to light (awareness) and perceive what is there (truth). Our eyes are organs of truth. When we have difficulty dealing with the subjective truth of what we see or don't see, we may reflect this to ourselves with trouble in our eyes.

Because our left eye is symbolic of feminine energy and our right eye of masculine energy, our left eye indicates how we "see" our relationships to Beingness, self-love, creativity, receiving and women (mothers, sisters, relatives, wives, friends and other females). Our right eye reflects how we "see" our relationship to Doingness, assertiveness, self-esteem, giving, men (fathers, brothers, relatives, husbands, friends and other males) and the world.

There are several disturbances we can create and locate in our eyes. The most common problem seems to be myopia, a contraction of muscles which either shortens or lengthens our eyeball, inducing difficulty in seeing objects close by (farsightedness) or far away (nearsightedness). Myopia usually indicates fear. Farsightedness indicates a fear of focusing on the truth of what is close by - - impacts created by ourselves, our family and/or society. Farsightedness can also be chosen out of an angry refusal to look at and give to our immediate environment (re: the "sit down strike" discussed in Chapter Two). Nearsightedness indicates a fear of seeing what is ahead, in our future. It may also indicate an anger about not having what we want now, thus refusing to look into the future.

The degree of eye difficulty can indicate secondary gains of avoiding responsibility, getting attention, pity or even punishment. Disturbances, which block out sight temporarily or permanently, may be selected because of a strong desire to not be aware of a subjective truth about ourselves or others. Problems with sight, since that is such a heavy experience, may also be chosen as a Lifetime's framework, to redirect our vision, to encourage the development of our inner resources, spiritual vision and growth.

OUR EARS

Our ears are divided into three sections; outer, middle and inner. Our outer ears are parabolic, trumpet-like, sound collecting extensions of our inner ears. Our middle ear serves to amplify the collected sound energy and convert it into mechanical energy. In the inner ear this mechanical energy is amazingly refined into electrical impulses which are then transmitted to our brain to be interpreted. Our brain actually knows nothing of sound, but only of energetic "bites" that it relates to. Our inner ears are also in charge of spatial orientation and balance. Because many cultures have encouraged meditation and use of inner senses, ears have long been considered a sacred organ. As one can see in one's mind, so can one hear. The psychic use of hearing is called clairaudience.

Psychologically speaking, disease or injury to our ears indicates a desire to not hear what has been or could be said. The usual emotions involved are hurt, anger or fear (often of further hurt). Right or left ear indicates the sex of the people from whom the message is not wanted.

For instance, from my own experience, at the time when I was first confronting inferiority and fear of rejection from women, I was on my way to a nearby island for an Indian pow-pow. I saw a woman I was attracted to taking the ferry with me and pondered talking to her, but felt afraid. I hemmed and hawed just enough so that the opportunity to approach her passed. Approximately four minutes later I was amazed that I actually began to feel an intense pain in my left ear. I immediately realized this body signal indicated my fear of hearing her assumed rejection and then set about to deal with fear of rejection and my lagging self-image.

OUR BRAIN

The primary body organ of spiritual evolution is our brain. There are a few salient metaphysical ideas to clarify about our beautiful brains. First, our brain is the physical counterpart to our non-physical mind. This is why our brains house the two most etheric chakras, the sixth (pituitary) and the seventh (pineal). These chakra centers are responsible for the energies of higher Human functioning: psychic abilities and mystical experiences. These chakras are the cup of love into which our consciousness first pours our Life energy so we can maintain our beautiful body. Disease or injury to our brain is sometimes tricky to interpret because the brain is responsible for everything that occurs in our body. Therefore, look at the function(s) impaired and analyze according to the principles already mentioned. Because we use our brains to think, brain damage often indicates a conscious or unconscious desire to not think anymore, to not be aware, to not be responsible; a desire to, in essence, become numb. Also and contrariwise, there are those of us who rely on our thinking way too much and, in a manner of speaking, try to live our Lives through our brains. We try to intellectualize our feelings away and easily get "stuck in our heads" (re: the "long neck" style referred to earlier). Since anger, guilt, sadness and other emotions cannot be thought away, we may locate a disturbance in our brains to indicate a collection and festering of energy which needs to be released through our guts, not our brains; this dynamic especially applies to tumors in the brain. Other motives for placing difficulties in our brain may relate to a desire to hold ourselves back from thinking, to win someone's approval ("You're stupid, Kid." "Ok, Dad."), to punish ourselves for thoughts considered wrong or to end our Lifetime quickly or to martyrishly, slowly fade brainlessly away.

SUMMARY

BODY PARTS AND CHAKRAS

FIRST CHAKRA	SECOND CHAKRA	THIRD CHAKRA
Anus, Buttocks	Testes	Adrenal Glands
Coccyx Bone	Ovaries	Kidneys
Lower Spine	Penis	Stomach
Bones	Vagina	Liver
Feet	Clitoris	Pancreas
Calves	Cervix	Gall Bladder
Thighs	Fallopian Tubes	Spleen
Tongue	Breasts	Small Intestine
Forearms	Hip Bones	Large Intestine
	Teeth	Lungs
	Wrists	Mid Back
	Ankles	
	Tongue	
	Eyes	
	Ears	
	Nose	
	Knees	
	Elbows	

FOURTH CHAKRA   FIFTH CHAKRA

Thymus Gland	Thyroid Gland	Pharynx
Heart	Parathyroid	Cervical Vertebrae
Ribs	Throat	Shoulders
Chest	Larynx	Jaw
Upper Back	Tongue	Eyes
	Teeth	Ears
		Nose

SIXTH CHAKRA   SEVENTH CHAKRA

Pituitary	Pineal Gland
Brain	Brain
Overall Effects	Overall Effects

In this chapter, we have discussed the Human body from toe to head and I hope you now have a better idea of what is happening in the moment to moment creation of our beautiful, communicative bodies. In Chapter Four we will discuss several physical conditions that will further illustrate and tie together these very fine principles of Body Symbolism.

CHAPTER FOUR

DISEASE EXAMPLES

In this chapter we will discuss the mechanisms and motives of heredity, cancer, auto-immune diseases and other interesting (and heart-breaking) varieties of illness. The focus of this chapter is to further illustrate how our emotional concerns are purposefully, resourcefully communicated through our body. Again, please remember that different people may have different emotional motives for creating the same body condition. I write with love and compassion as I explain these dynamics. I feel for you if you or those you love have or will have these wretched conditions. As you read on, please remember that healing is available at any moment; even yesterday, since there is no time. Truly, my thoughts and heart are with you.

MELODRAMA

Melodrama is an important experience to clarify because it relates heavily to manifesting all kinds of negative conditions in our

Lives. Little is written about melodrama as it concerns disease and injury creation. Melodrama is an attitude of theatrics - - a belief in the value of and a desire for the flair of histrionic show.

We easily understand and accept that something as simple as an automobile has various components that make it work. We do not yet widely understand or accept that a being as complex as a Human also has various components that make him work. Nor do we widely understand that some of these parts are unhealthy, even deadly to our well-being. This is a very important, huge topic which I will explore and explain in a future book. For now, though, you might read everything you can get about Transactional Analysis, as explained in the early best-seller, *I'm Ok, You're Ok,* by Thomas Harris. It better suits our purposes now, however, to simplify this quest for understanding and just discuss the most dangerous, most toxic aspects attached to being a Human.

The melodramatic side of us stems in part from our Adapted Child, a part of us which seeks negative attention because he thinks that's all he deserves and that's the only way he can get any notice at all. This is the part of us that got brainwashed into thinking we are unworthy. The more disdain and punishment we received from "out there," the more we turned it on ourselves and disliked ourselves "in here." Well, this is the part of us that believes in and carries our shame. Shame is the most powerful, most unhealthy experience Humans have. We all have it. We all have it. How sad. How shameful.

There is, however, an equally insidious component that is not us, but is attached to us. It needs special explanation and clarification. This is the real enemy. This is the *real* demon. It is The Terrorist Within.

TERRORISM IS OUTSIDE US BECAUSE WE DO NOT YET KNOW HOW TO SEE IT WITHIN US.

It is our Negative Ego. In order to unmask its cruel activity, we would do well to first discuss its counterpart, The Positive Ego. This will help clarify the damaging game of melodrama as a motive for disease and injury selection.

Every person has an ego, each varying in maturity, strength and ability to function. The ego is a psychic apparatus that regulates our mental functions of perception, assessment and identity boundaries. The ego's primary job is to mediate a healthful balance between our two realms of activity: between our inner, PSYCHE creativity and our outer, TECHNE impacts on our physical environment. Our ego's main role is to tell us what we are creating "out there" so we can make decisions "in here" whether or not we want to keep the creations. Our ego's job is to tell us what we see. It is the part of us that first assess what is presently around us.

For instance, if we create and look at a blue street lamp, our ego's job is to assess what is physically there and communicate it in thought to our non-physical mind: "There is a street lamp. It is blue." Because many of us do not yet know or trust our non-physical natures (our emotional, psychic and spiritual components), we deny them and thereby unconsciously load onto our ego duties that it is incapable of handling well. One such duty is making emotional judgments about the objects or events we see. Our egos function best when they report physical inventory, but not manage our mental store; when they report physical data, but not suggest judgments about that data. The balanced ego, the one that simply reports information of what is around us, can be referred to as "The Positive Ego". When we are dangerously out of sync with our true selves, when we will not think, feel or intuit for ourselves (often conditioned out of us in our (Adapted) childhoods, we give our egos too much of a burden and unconsciously ask them to interpret objects and events in our Lives, rather than just report them. We, in effect, ask our Positive Ego to not only tell us what is there (reporting information), but we also ask it how we feel about it (making emotional judgments: Is it good or bad ? Do we like it or not?).

This arrests our ego's development. The ego, in effect, goes into shock and splits into two; one Positive and one immature or Negative. This is unconscious on our part, yet it still happens. The Positive Ego gets sort of weak and the Negative Ego rises up and to face the burdening challenge. It takes charge of making emotional judgments it never really wanted to do in the first place. It was designed to just report that the blue street lamp is out there, *not* write an essay about its significance to us!

Our Negative Ego, in effect, gets pissed off and vows to seek revenge against us for giving it too much work. Since it cannot physically hurt us because it is a mental apparatus, it vows to talk *us* into hurting ourselves by ruining our Lives. It does this by suggesting in our thoughts that we ought to feel *sorry* for ourselves. It chooses this weapon because self-pity is poison, absolute *poison*, to our spirituality !!!

Our spirituality is our love or ourselves, our Lives and Goddess-God. We <u>cannot</u> feel love if we are choosing pity! We cannot expand in our hearts if we are contracting in our guts. Our Negative Egos are on a mission of revenge and have as their only goal talking us into ruining our Lives by turning our self-pitying backs on ourselves, each other and Goddess-God. It tells us we are victims and martyrs. It tries to get us to play "better than" or "worse than" games. To think we are better than or worse than any other person creates separation and isolation. The Negative Ego then uses this self-selected pain to justify more self-pity ("Ahhh, poor me I'm so cool and I have to live among all these lower Life forms." Or: "Poor me, I am not as good as they are." Or: "Poor me, I have so much to do......my Life is such a burden.").

The opposite of pity is gratitude. The Negative Ego *hates* gratitude. It will continually suggest in our thoughts that we are misunderstood, taken advantage of, unappreciated and have problems that are horrible, terrible and awful (poor us) ….. all with

no solutions (poor us again). Therefore, we cannot, *absolutely*

cannot feel gratitude! So what if we can see, hear, talk, walk, act,

live outside a war zone or have shoes? After all, we have big

problems! It pushes and pushes us to shun gratitude and choose

self-pity, knowing this will only lead to more self-pity. Get this:

prolonged wallowing in pity thoughts and feelings will go out and

interact with The Great Principle Of Reflectivity and bring back

exactly what we offered: more pitiful events! Then feel sorry for

ourselves about those? Hell, we will attract even more pitiful

events, which can lead to an eventual collapse of our reality (hell).

This ugly, disgusting, demon-like Negative Ego is in all of us. It is

in *ALL* of us! There is *NOTHING* good about the Negative Ego!

Our Negative Egos are the ultimate self-defeating, terrorist

part of Humanity. Only recently have we had these dynamics made

clear to us by Lazaris. Only recently have we been made aware of

the existence of our Negative Ego and its perverse pity-seeking

games of victimhood and martyrhood. Victims are those people

who always lose at everything or almost everything. They suffer,

snort up a lot of pity and complain loudly about their ill-fated Lives

("Life's a bitch"). Martyrs do their pity differently. Martyrs always suffer. They don't thrive, they survive. They sigh a lot, and think or actually say "Why bother?" They also deny responsibility for their Lives and impacts, even surpassing some of the most die-hard victims. Martyrs don't want to hear solutions; they would rather tell you why your idea won't work and why they are stuck in their pitiful mess (poor them). People who play Victim and Martyr listen to their Negative Egos frequent suggestions of hopelessness in their thoughts. Unfortunately, no one has taught them to rebuke these false thoughts and change their feelings (please remember: thoughts create feelings. If we do not like how we are feeling, we must examine and change our thoughts). Thank Goddess, we are finally catching on to this *most destructive* aspect of Human nature! There is nothing good about the Negative Ego. Everyone has one. It thinks in our thoughts, like an "alien" (that is why the movie, *The Alien* was so popular; it was a depiction of what each of us is dealing with in a fight for (spiritual) survival against an ugly, rabid beast inside us that only cares for its own agenda of us having a terrible Life or a terrible death). To influence this self-sabotage, our

Negative Egos suggest to us self-defeating thoughts and self-harming and other-harming acts. We must all learn about this harmful component attached to ourselves so we can rebuke its negative, ugly games of seeking self-pity and excuses for that pity.

Get this: the Negative Ego is the experience from which the metaphor of the devil in the bibles was created! Yes, we each have our own personal "devil" that seeks to tempt us into harmful, really sinful, thoughts of better than (which is BIGOTRY), worse than, hopelessness and pity! When we finally wake up to our spirituality and want our Negative Ego to grow up and go away, it fights to retain the dominant position in our thought, which we previously gave it. It becomes the fallen ruler who will not give up the thrown. Ha, how many times has this drama been acted of the world stage, with the many world despots taking their turn at this (Mephisto) role?

Thus, instead of simply viewing and reporting the blue street lamp so we can enjoy it cleanly, the Negative Ego takes over and extrapolates in our thinking: "There is a street lamp. It is blue. Because I appreciate its blue beauty, I am more sensitive than others and therefore I am better than others who do not study and appreciate this marvelous street lamp. I am more aware, aesthetically oriented, intelligent and more enriched than they. I sure like myself because I am so much better than them. Poor me (sigh) I'm all alone in my high ability, sigh, to appreciate beauty."

Or, our Negative Ego could suggest thoughts in the other (false and destructive) direction: "Wow, I'm such a shmuck! Here I have been passing this blue street lamp every day and just now noticed it? What a jerk I am; oh so much less aware than others, less evolved, not as good as others! Damn, I missed out. Must be my defective genes. Poor me."

Instead of just reporting the data, you see, our Negative Ego goes for self-inflation or self-debasement and runs our thoughts in directions of pitiful, spiritual error. The core spiritual truth, of course, is that no one, no piece of Life, is better than or worse than any other piece of Life on the inside. We just have different talents and capacities on the outside.

Also, our Negative Egos, if we let them, can go similarly whacko in the creation of bodily disturbances. To better justify throwing our Lives away, so we may more comfortably disintegrate into hopelessness-pity (again, poor us), our Negative Ego suggests in our thoughts that we are victims and cannot win, no matter what or how hard we try. We are dead in the water. It tells us we are weak and extremely powerless in the face of bumps in the road, especially illness. Since many of us unfortunately fall for this lie that we are not powerful, cannot win and be happy ("Life sucks - - poor me"), we swallow hard and think we might as well settle in Life for some dose of "hard reality". Thus, we mistakenly say yes to our Negative Ego's suggestions and thereby force our Free Child Within, who seeks aliveness and fun, into dormancy. Because so many of us do not feel our worth-power or joy (our Adapted Child), we often sink to the lowest level and seek a sense of aliveness, *pseudo-importance* and pseudo-nurturing through arrogance and pity. I think this is why soap operas, macho crap and gangsta-rap-toughness are so popular; they represent the melodramatic part of us, acted out in grand, melodramatic scenarios of struggle.

Applied to the topic of this book, the melodramatic approach to disease creation sounds like this:

"Welllll, I de-value and dislike myself quite a lot, have a lot of anger repressed over the years, feel like I am drowning in it and would like to punish myself. Yep, sounds about right. I'll roll all of these into one big, communicative mess and give myself a lung condition like bronchitis. No, wait; not enough. I have really been rotten and I really, really dislike myself and I have suffered so very much in the past - - nobody knows the trouble I've seen - - so, sure, I'll just show them all! Right, my Life is so hard, so much harder than theirs', so I will go all the way and do emphysema! Yeah, that way people will know that I really am having a hard Life that I am better than them at being worse than. I am better than them at struggle, at being unhealthy; I'm really drowning. Ok, cancel that measly bronchitis and cue the emphysema!"

Here is another example of Negative Ego melodrama acted out through injuring our beloved body: "I have a fear of reaching out for nourishment because my mother and father never liked me depending on them to meet my needs and they often rebuked me when I was the most needy. I am going to communicate this fear and attendant rage to myself by breaking my right, reaching-for arm. That should do it. No, wait. I'll let them all know how much I feel afraid - - how very, very afraid I feel - - I will not only break my arm, I'll have it crushed! Yes, yes that should let them and me know just how very, very, very afraid and angry I feel and how absolutely terrible and horrible and powerless my Life has been since those bad, terrible people did all those horrible acts to me and made me such a powerless, defenseless, poor down-trodden, pitiful creature, all against my own, powerless will. I want to show them how they totally, totally messed up my poor, miserable Life, poor me. I'll show them, yes, I'll really show them! My hyper-suffering will show how special my problems are (poor me again). Now, where is my arm-crushing truck?"

Some of the above may be overstated a bit, but, unfortunately, not by much for far too many of us. Our Negative Ego has a melodramatic investment in our suffering through upping the severity of a Life problem, including disease and injury - - all the better (than) to attract national attention, gather pity and play the false, self-defeating roles of "better than" or "worse than" through victimhood and martyrhood.

Most everyone has "done time" in these roles; they can feel like prison! Let he who is without such error cast a better than, bigoted stone, not those of us who are busy authentically growing and stretching (and inevitably stumbling). Let us instead show compassion, much compassion. We must keep in mind that if we are involved with people and/or ourselves who have Negative Ego investments in having problems, we would do well to approach them and us kindly. Suffering can be a real drag to be around; that is true and it is ok to feel angry about it, but it is not ok to use our anger as an excuse to hurt someone, or ourselves. That is a total lack of spiritual responsibility and it is disgustingly mean. It would be much better instead to communicate our feelings in an emotionally honest, non-hurtful way, always encouraging self and others toward personal respect, growth and creativity (perhaps encourage psychotherapy - - one of the nicest gifts we could give ourselves - - when it is done well).

Our Negative Egos may not use disease, injury or personal suffering to establish our false better thans. We may use other equally specious proofs, such as nice looks, money, education, talent, lineage, popularity, money, hurdles overcome, etc. Better than (the core idea of bigotry) is a very common and very injurious game, one we need to be most vigilant against. Our Negative Egos like to suggest in our thoughts the most self-defeating, hopeless ideas possible, hoping we will buy into its pity-ploy (that is all it is capable of suggesting to us). It hopes we will discount our current successes, beauty and fun and then throw these gems of consciousness onto the trash heap of "taking ourselves for granted" (a deadly practice our culture encourages). Handling our destructive Negative Egos is a full time job at first. With much practice at repeatedly telling it to shut up in our thoughts, we can master it and then learn to release its game. Then we can learn to help it grow up, transform its energy and blend it into our Positive Ego.

This is a beautiful experience I have had good success with. My Negative Ego was a killer before I healed it. It would suggest all kinds of stupid lies to me in my thoughts. Lies about me not being good enough, not being competent enough, being a failure when my income was very low, being a loser, etc. Once, when I was standing on a bridge, my Negative Ego even suggested that I jump off, just for the heck of it! How insane! Once I became aware of its nature and games, I had to do a lot of self-talk to repeatedly rebuke its pity messages and not go down those thought-roads. I had to resist the temptation to indulge in the pity-party that I had become used to. I had to fight the old way of thinking and feeling and assert my worth, talent and consciously wallow in my gratitudes. I hung onto my gratitudes like a shipwrecked person hangs onto driftwood! I mean, I knew it was my survival that was at stake! I had to give up the pity. With much practice I got my head above water and then, after battling my Negative Ego, I began to love it.

Yes, I began to love it back to health. In meditation I let it tell me all of the ways I had hurt it, how I had blamed it for my shortcomings and failures. I then let it express its anger at me for doing so. This may sound nuts to some, or a lot, of you, but I swear this *is* a legitimate, therapeutic process to heal one's ego. When its anger was drained, I began the truthful process of apologizing for my mistakes and telling it that it was good. My ego never let me down. I just blamed it because I was in pain. I took this cruelty off my ego's shoulders with repeated appreciations. After all, my ego got me through my Life to the point where I was then. That was good success! I let it know that, over and over. I heaped appreciations and commendations on it throughout my daily activities.

Over time, my ego became less rabid and more tame. Eventually it became an ally and a friend. I think my Positive Ego has been rescued from the trash bin of undeserved blame and shame and shined up, healed into a wonderfully Positive Ego state. I talk to my Positive Ego every day (unless I forget, which he does not like) and tell it how much I appreciate its success in informing me of my previous day's events.

This healing process is delineated in Lazaris' tapes about healing The Negative Ego. I would strongly, strongly, strongly recommend them to everyone. They sure worked for me.

Again, the basic spiritual truth is that, as far as inner worth is concerned, no one is ever better than or worse than any other. The sooner we "grok" this core truth of Life, the sooner we stop playing stupid Negative Ego games of better than, less than, hopelessness and self-pity.

Please do yourselves the favor of re-reading this section on Melodrama as often as you need to, so you can better understand your Negative Egos' nature and games. Your Negative Ego will tell you: "Naw, you don't really need to re-read; you understand everything, so just go on." Right. Please don't fall for that line. It wants to remain invisible to you so it can better sabotage you in your thoughts. Will you re-read? I hope so.

HEREDITY

On the physical level, heredity is the process of distributing physical (and some would say mental-emotional) characteristics from the parents' cells to the child's cells. This is accomplished through duplication and division of the parents' combined DNA. As you probably know, DNA (Deoxyribonucleic Acid) is our atomic blueprint for all cell structure and activity. The child's first cell, his zygote, inherits 23 units of DNA-chromosomes from each parent, for a total of 46. The chromosomes and DNA mix and match according to certain principles; the study of which is the field of genetics.

According to the metaphysical view of Life, we are alive when we are "dead"; that is, not inhabiting a body. We are alive in another level of reality, not the physical. Here are some incredibly important ideas which will change the way we relate to our and others' Lives forever: when a spirit decides to have a physical go-at-it and begin another Lifetime, we must make several important decisions. We decide what we want as a psychological and spiritual focus for this Lifetime. We decide which pocket of space and time we want to inhabit and who we want to be our parents, siblings and relatives. We also decide which sex we prefer to be this Lifetime, which race we prefer, which sexual orientation we prefer and how we want our body to look and function! If the spirit desires a negative condition to symbolize or provide a growth issue, we will program it into the DNA code of the fetus we create and will soon inhabit.

When we choose a hereditary disease, a physical appearance or a condition that favors one parent above the other, we do so to more closely align ourselves with that parent (or sibling). Parent-child similarity is not a result of the mechanics of genetics, but instead, occurs as a result of the metaphysical dynamic of heredity - - to resonate as fully as we can, to imitate to the depth of our genetic code, the parent we want to love and be loved by the most! Or it could be because we want to emulate the qualities of that parent. Of course, this genetic imitation fits in perfectly with our growth plan for this Lifetime or else it would not be occurring because we would not choose it.

Another motive to consider for a genetic disease is the following: sometimes we plan a Lifetime out of beliefs and desires that are rather limiting. For instance, if we acted horribly manipulative or cruel in a previous Lifetime (a mistake we have all made in cultivating our growth), we may die feeling guilty or ashamed of ourselves. Or, we may die still believing in Karma, an Eastern concept that says if we messed up now, we must pay back or redeem ourselves with suffering in our next Lifetime.

You see, after we die we go to another reality and inspect the Life we have just lived (the "Day Of Judgment" referred to in the bible). We evaluate our thoughts and actions with scorching honesty and may become intently disgusted with ourselves if we find we have (again) betrayed our spiritual growth. On top of that, if we have hurt other people, very deep disappointment in self can result which can feel like hell, a horrible hell. Well, some of us feel so badly about ourselves that we try to (unnecessarily) "make it up" to Humanity, ourselves or our relatives by having a difficult Life our next time. So, we may arrange a Lifetime in which we enter with a deformed body and/or have a condition that requires suffering, like spina bifida or rickets. The parents of this person, of course, have chosen to participate in this drama for their own belief-emotional reasons.

I know this explanation is difficult for some of us to accept. We have a large prejudice because of our limited, linear chronological perspective which says: "How can anyone, let alone a little, tiny baby be responsible for what happens to him? After all, his Life just started."

I realize this perceptual shift may be difficult at first, especially when some heavy emotions are involved, but metaphysics says that baby is no baby; that is, not an empty slate to be written upon by this, his first Life. That "baby", like you and I, is a time and space traveler, an Earth-visiting entity with perhaps thousands of years of growth experience accrued already.

My non-physical friend Lazaris, for instance, says that most of us alive now were around during the third civilization of Atlantis (approximately 10,800 B.C.). We have come back in this pocket of space-time because we do not like what we experienced then (wretched cataclysmic destruction through heavy investments in doom and gloom). Now we want to get things right (i.e. playful) and influence events so that mass destruction does not happen again, especially now that we have the nonsense of nuclear, biological and pollution negativity. So good to get it right this time (yes!) and as spiritual adults choose growth, cooperation, harmony and peace, individually and en masse.

So, the next time you see a baby, think about who and where that baby might have been before. And out of respect for his vast consciousness (and yours), please do not play those ugly, ego-authoritarian games with him, such as: "I'm the adult, you're the kid and I'm better than you."

CANCER

Cancer is one of the most feared body conditions in our culture. Other cultures in history have had their most feared conditions, too. Let's see: there was small pox, malaria, Black Plague, tuberculosis, influenza, pneumonia, diphtheria and even childbirth. With modern medical treatments, however, Humanity has pretty much stopped these disease conditions from leading to death (of course, we are always free to choose a "resurgence" of these).

Recently we have come to rely rather heavily upon an old mode of exit, cancer. I am very sure that if we do find a medical cure for cancer, we will increase our exiting via another condition or else create a brand-new "killer disease", as we did when we generated AIDS. When we Humans want to exit, come hell or high water or medical science, we will exit.

Many substances have been suggested as being causes of cancer: from pajamas, to bacon, to fluoridated water, to alcohol, even bruises, as well as dioxin and other ugly, seriously poisonous chemicals (cigarettes). To deal with our great concern about cause and treatment, billions of dollars are spent each year on research, particularly in laboratories and hospitals, with an unfortunate sub-pittance of funding going toward research through psychotherapy (hopefully, this will change soon). I am all in favor of the efforts of the thousands of people who raise money for cancer research through races, walks, bake sales, lemonade sales, etc. I think these are greatly loving. Scientific research may indeed lead to a breakthrough to stop the physical craziness that is cancer. I sure hope so. If we did have that cure, though, we would still have to look at the underlying, emotional reasons why we chose the condition in the first place. Let us not lose sight of that, please.

Many physicians and researchers, from Galen in 180 A.D. to Paget in 1870, to LeShan in 1965, to Silva in 1971, to the Simontons in 1975 have studied and written about people who have cancer conditions. They seem to have identified the major emotional components of cancer creation, but these have not yet been accepted by our medical establishment or our populace. I hope to shed a bit of light on how emotional factors create cancer and why healing treatments, conventional or not, can fail.

Cancer is just like any other disease condition; it is purposely chosen, has definite emotional roots and can be reversed as desired. Let us look at what the condition of cancer is: it is a group of cells that are freeloading. For yet medically unexplained reasons, one's cells begin to multiply crazily. The most harmful effect of this is that the new cells do not do any work. They are like parasites that do not contribute to the homeostatic balance of our body. In fact, they ravage the body's equilibrium as they suck up needed food, interfere with crucial chemical processes and /or strangle affected or near-by organs. Not very kind at all, but very purposeful.

Cancer symbolizes two experiences: the first is the accumulation of too much emotional energy in our system. This is especially symbolized by tumors; too much mass in the body, just as there is too much emotional mass in our system (the emotional mass was created first).

The second experience symbolized by cancer relates to a deep desire for a change in our Lives. Cancer indicates we are miserable with the conditions of our Lives or how we are living our Lives. This is especially represented by the freeloading action of the cancer cells. When we live in a way that does not honor our Child Within, when we try to hide from our emotions, when we sacrifice our spirit to duty, obligation, doingness and appearance, we can feel awfully empty. Often we try to hide from our feelings. When we over-burden ourselves with excess emotional baggage we can feel tired, helpless and sometimes hopeless. When we burden ourselves with unexpressed emotion to the extent of feeling awfully tired, helpless and hopeless, we may desire to change our Lives, even give it all up and just "freeload" for a while. Non-productive cells represent our inner desire to not have to produce anymore, in essence to regress, to be taken care of because of too many emotional burdens, too much emotional energy stuck in our system. The primary emotion motivating a cancerous condition is anger; anger that is repressed, locked up and accumulated into a large mass with no place to go - - no way out.

When we create and bottle up anger and then keep on stuffing new angers into our system, we are being mean to ourselves. Plus, we are living like a martyr because we are burdening ourselves (poor me) unnecessarily. We Humans, you see, have designed ourselves just like beings who live in the vaster, more intense planes of existence; we all function through emotion. The more expanded beings "out there" are centered around emotion; they eat emotion, fly through emotion and they interpenetrate emotionally. We Humans do these emotional acts, too, except on a smaller, less intense scale so we can slowly acclimate and learn to handle the intensity of emotion. We, like those beings, are designed to let our emotions flow through us, through our beautiful skin, out into the atmosphere. To repress our feelings is to fight our Human essence, to fight Nature, the TAO. Interesting to note, Taoism, a philosophy from ancient China, extols the properties of flowing water as an analogy of living fully, harmoniously in Life. As mentioned in Chapter Two, water in the Earth, our body, dreams, Tarot, much mythology and astrology symbolizes emotion. Thus, to be in harmony with our deepest nature (i.e. the TAO) we need to honestly, emotionally flow, like water.

Unfortunately, our Paradigm Two, distorted masculine energy, dominating, macho, arrogant, materialistic society encourages self-deception and alienation through emotional repression, so many of us get brainwashed into fighting our true selves. This sort of spiritual slop never washes with our Soul or our Inner Child's true desire for enlightened, creative expansion. And, because there is no time in the realm of emotion and because emotion is cumulative, we cannot do this self-denial too long without some adverse effects, without some knock-knock from our inner selves that we're a messin' up our emotional-spiritual growth. As mentioned, we often knock with bodily disturbances.

In treating cancer, we would do well to focus on anger and hate. Now, anger and hate, like our other emotions, are totally innocent and want nothing more than to go outside and play in the air. There is nothing wrong, perverted or dangerous about anger or its more intense version, hate. This is a most important point. As mentioned in Chapter Two, what is not ok is how some of us express our feelings of anger and hate, namely violence. Prohibit violence and then hate with gusto, is my motto.

Please remember, the golden rule of emotional health is: If we create an emotion, we need to express that emotion, with harm to none. Hate is created when our desire to love is blocked and frustrated and we feel repeated angers. We would not feel hate if we did not want to love and be close. We would not go to the trouble of creating hate if the person or desired experience (like societal harmony) was not so wanted and loved. When we want to be close and we are not allowed to, we feel pain, the pain of separation. Repeated pains and angers naturally accumulate into hate. That's ok. The denial of this hate, however, is not ok; it is incredibly damaging to us. Hate is a very intense anger that, if communicated well (i.e. non-violently), can unblock channels to allow the love to flow again. Sometimes it is quite appropriate to hate our mothers, fathers, wives, husbands, children, sisters, brothers, grandparents, peers or dishes. Rather than try to banish hate, we would do much better to learn how to healthfully release it once we have created it. Creating hate unnecessarily or irrationally, of course, is to be avoided. The likelihood of giving ourselves beautiful, expanding fourth chakra feelings of self-love, joy, peace and fun rests upon a foundation of willingness to honestly experience our third chakra, contracting feelings of anger, fear, sadness, disappointment, etc. Two sides to a coin, you know; the TAO is the whole and balance is handling both sides well.

Those of us who deny ourselves the great liberation of releasing feelings of hate (with harm to none) will also deny ourselves the great liberation of truly forgiving the offending person(s). We will thus stick ourselves with much stagnant energy in our systems. Keep piling anger on top of anger, on top of anger and after a while, there is so much pressure locked up inside that it can seem like it is just too, too much to bear. So much so that we inwardly get to feeling hopeless, like we are going to either explode or, worse, just fade away.

When we create cancer we often feel a smothering sense of hopelessness because of our stockpiled anger and limiting beliefs and we may, in effect, want to quit and just "freeload" for a while. LeShan and other researchers have found that most cancer patients they studied had "distressing" (i.e. unloving, even violent) relationships with one or more parents. This is likely when they started to stockpile their anger and hate and, unfortunately, continued until they manifested their cancerous conditions. Those of us who give ourselves cancer usually feel angry at ourselves, too, not just because of the cancer, but for how we lived before the cancer, usually with a poor self-image, little self-love and wasted time.

A cancer condition is a call home - - home to our emotional authenticity, respect, honesty and freedom; all achieved through responsibility, love and clean communication. Heeding this call back to self, we can start Life anew and have another Lifetime within the framework of this one! Our new Life can be much better than our previous one; this time strongly centered in actualizing our true self, our wonderfully precious Child Within.

And this is the glory of The New Age: that we understand Human dynamics to such a greater extent than ever before and can better educate to re-decide the priorities and course of our Lives, society and world. Where we locate our cancer indicates who and what our anger relates to. We will discuss some important considerations for healing in Chapter Five.

CANCER AND CHILDREN

I can just imagine what some of you are thinking now. Something like: "This metaphysical approach to disease creation and location may be acceptable when it comes to adults, but it is a lot harder to apply to children. Given what was just written about heredity and all that before-birth-stuff, it still is difficult to allow for a cute, little child actually choosing such a horrible disease as cancer. What about their innocence? Are they purposely creating leukemia, brain tumors, cerebral palsy, cystic fibrosis, spinal meningitis and other horrible problems? Innocent little kids? C'mon, you're kidding???"

I also thought this when I was first learning about metaphysics, so I can easily understand any incredulity. I feel so much for kids who are sick, like I would just love to take the hurt away and somehow instantly make them whole again (and there are some healers who can actually help do that). I feel a lot of compassion for parents who have children who are ill and I sincerely wish them a lot of strength and love as they deal with their feelings and difficulties. Yes, metaphysical principles are operative for each person on the planet, no matter what their chronological age.

I would like to discuss eleven basic reasons why children give themselves catastrophic, Lifetime threatening diseases. Of course, no child sits down with his building blocks, cars or dolls and consciously decides to rearrange his blood composition so that he has one more year to live here. But decisions like this are indeed made on inner levels by this Lifetimes-old, inner maturing entity who currently looks like a child. The decisions when and how to end his Lifetime are his to make and his alone. Same for you and I.

It is so very difficult for any sensitive person to be involved with anyone who is suffering, especially a child. This next section addresses the concerns of those who have or have had or will have a child who has a fatal illness or injury, particularly cancer.

In my work as a psychotherapist, I have dealt with people who have experienced tragic events with their children; injuries, diseases and deaths. I am a bit acquainted with the pain many feel, though I have not felt it myself because I do not have children this Lifetime. I hated to watch my dear friend die of cancer, though. The most difficult issues we face in our Lifetime can be understanding and accepting the suffering or death of those we love.

So often we blame ourselves for a loved one's misfortune. "If only I had done this" or "if only I had not gone there" or "If only... if only.... if only...." Loving, well intentioned as we are, we can put ourselves through absolute hell for real or imagined errors. The corridor to hell is lined with blame, guilt and self-punishment. The corridor to hell is lined with blame, guilt and self-punishment. These do us no good, my friends. These do us no healing.

For those of us who are parents, the burdens of guilt can be elevated to crisis, mind-blowing proportions. Since each entity chooses our own experience, it is important to discuss reasons *why* we would give ourselves a Life threatening disease, such as cancer. I am aware of eleven reasons I hope will help in understanding why children attract devastating diseases.

The first three reasons for a child to create a catastrophic disease have to do with influences received from parents. This discussion seeks to not blame parents, but to illume the ultra-influential relationship parents have with children, including the sad possibility of guiding kids into negative experiences, though unintended. Because of the very nature of the Human parenting relationship, a successful parent is required to be mature and in charge of his fears.

If a parent greatly fears injury or disease may happen to his child and worries and worries and talks and talks about it and worries and talks some more, he is not acting as a good parent right then. If a parent histrionically, melodramatically lays his fears on a child, the child may feel obliged to act out those fears for the parent's benefit - - to prove the parent "right", as it were. The child's thinking sounds something like: "Daddy, you talk an awful lot about bad things, even violence. Sometimes you even do violence. Well, I want you to love me, so I will help you get what you are always talking about because that must be what you want, I guess. And Mommy tells me, too. I want your approval so very much. Ok, Daddy-Mommy, I will get hit by a car, or kidnapped, or break my leg, or get really sick, or .....".

The second way disease or injury can be helped along by parents is through promoting a belief in the value of suffering and victimhood. Some kids have learned and strongly believe that living as a bloody victim is the road to spiritual glory, the only way to develop character, the only way to get God's love, the only way to be a true artist or even the *normal* course of events on this "evil" and "treacherous" planet. If a child believes these or other such negative (and false) ideas, he may select, through interaction with The Great Principle Of Reflectivity, a bunch of pain and misery.

The third influence parents could have on a child's decision to leave this Lifetime has to do with a strong desire to escape. We must note and vomit at the truth that millions of children are physically and emotionally battered every year. They are forced to endure horrible, horrible experiences and most of them have no way out. This disgusting cruelty may influence a child to quit this Lifetime and try again with better parents next time. A catastrophic disease or injury may actually be a gift from the child to himself, a way out of intolerable pain.

A personal note to parents: these are the only examples I know of in which parents are responsible for a child's mishaps. If you think you fit these descriptions, then please take it easy with yourselves. It is tragic, yes, because it might have been avoided. Please leave it there, do not add more tragedy to your Life or your child's Life with punishment of self or other. Your child needs you and you need you. Please do what you need to do to take good care of yourselves and your children as soon as possible; *change* your beliefs and behavior. Learn more of your value and the beauty of Life. Work with a good therapist (for several years) and please, please be kind to yourselves and your children. Only love heals.

Some parents have children who have created Lifetime-threatening diseases or injuries for other reasons. One such reason is the usual one for such an emotionally heavy experience - - to serve as a framework for growth. This may seem nuts to us at first because of all the suffering our child and us have gone through. Who the hell needs to grow that much or that way, right? Well, our child may have decided he needed that framework to suit his inner purposes. This choice may have been a good one for him - - fighting the disease may have given him the impetus to stretch and grow, to become freer in his love, wisdom and expression of self. Often children who are fighting against their disease or injury become teachers of love, acceptance and what is truly meaningful in Life for their parents and siblings. What wisdom does an entity bring into a Lifetime? Sometimes an encounter with a Life-threatening circumstance provides a forum from which the ancient ones can speak. That may sound nuts at first, but please ponder it.

As for the parents: as a tremendous gift to the child and as a framework of their own growth, they choose to serve as guides for the one who suffers as a child. They give themselves the gift of staying centered and strong in the face of great adversity; rejecting temptations of martyrhood and cynicism. These parents stay resolute in their commitment to seeing and loving the beauty of Life and Goddess-God. They do not succumb to their own dark-side when times are tough and, in fact, become stronger in their light-side as they may even help their child die with love of Life, dignity and ease.

A fifth reason for selecting cancer or a catastrophic injury involves the ol' standby mechanism of Body Symbolism. A child may create a bodily disturbance for the same reason an adult does - - to inform himself that a toxic accumulation of sadness, anger, victimhood, weakness or other emotion is in his system, even from another Lifetime (there is no time in the realm of emotion). Over-repressing emotion is detrimental to any Human, no matter what his chronological age.

A sixth reason for creating cancer or injury may be difficult to accept, but certainly must be considered. It is usually not the primary motive for choosing a Lifetime-threatening illness, but can be and can also cement the other motives into place rather strongly. This sixth reason is often referred to as "secondary gains". Specifically, this means a child chooses cancer or injury as a way to achieve emotional payoffs. A child, for instance, may desire more of our attention, comforting and closeness. He may choose and use his condition to secure himself a place in our family constellation and hopefully our hearts. This may seem rather extreme to us, but to a child who needs love, attention and security, it may inwardly make perfect sense and not at all be too much of a price to pay. This is especially so if his parents tend to be physically or emotionally cruel, unavailable or, so unfortunately, stingy with affection.

A child may also choose cancer or injury because he feels very unworthy, ashamed, guilty or self-hating. He may be punishing himself heavily with his condition: "I am so rotten, I can't do anything right. I am stupid and no good just like Mom or Dad said. I hate myself and deserve to be punished". Or, closely related, a child may sacrifice his health as a means to punish his parents: "There! Now I got you back for all that hurt you gave me! Now you have to take care of me and spend all your money and time on me and have no fun yourselves. Ha!" Or, a child may even create a negative condition as a means of giving his family a "central project" in hopes his parents will finally, finally stop fighting and stop being mean to each other. It is as if he was playing "wounded bird", drawing all the attention to himself to induce a cease fire from the combatants above so he can finally have a semblance of a secure home.

Primary in any of these experiences is the emotion of anger, either turned on oneself in the form of self-hate, guilt and punishment or anger turned on others in the form of revenge and punishment. Once again, the destructiveness of repressed anger highlights the crucial importance of allowing children to express their emotions, with harm to none. It also highlights the importance of meeting our responsibility of tending to our children, treating them and their feelings with respect and kindness so they do not need a calamity to get our attention or negotiate a truce from the hurtfulness, even brutality, of our stupid immaturity. To those who want health and healing in their households, this discussion points up the incredible value of entering family therapy because that is such an effective, practical forum for resolving the heavy emotional issues described on these pages.

The tenth reason I am aware of why some children give themselves cancer or traumatic injury is because of their belief in retribution. As discussed earlier, some of us believe we must pay a price for our misdeeds from another Lifetime and/or this Lifetime. We may choose congenital conditions that involve disfigurement or suffering or may elect to have cancer that goes through repeated stages of remission and exacerbation.

The final reason I am aware of for choosing a Lifetime-threatening disease or injury involves a desire to end this Lifetime. That death occurs when a child is very young seems unjust and brutally tragic to many parents. Most understandably, many feel ripped-off, enraged and stricken with grief. Many parents, unfortunately, start to blame and hate God or Life for making their dear, lovely child suffer or for taking their baby away from them. If not careful, these parents can generate and accumulate many mega-explosions of rage and cynicism in their guts and only hurt and their own hearts and realities further.

A child's death is incredibly painful to most parents. It is important to remember, however: a child's death is not unjust. Every individual has been given the gift of the gods - - to create his own experience. This Lifetime is like a chapter in an epic novel, one of many.

A Lifetime starts at the point of *entry* into the fetus (*not* conception !!!) and ends at the point of departure, death. We select our Lifetime's beginning, end and all the razz-ma-tazz in between. Cancer or other calamity may be a convenient avenue of departure for an entity to take, particularly if he wants to make a statement with his death, like pointing up the importance of living fully in the NOW and not taking the gift of Life for granted or highlighting our societal stupidity in dealing with toxic wastes.

We may want to stop a Lifetime at an early age because of two basic reasons. The first reason is that, once inside the structure of our Lifetime, we decide we made a mistake and do not want to proceed. We know that we will be alive somewhere else, as we were before we created and inhabited this body, so we switch our focus of intent and operation. Of course, we take into account the effect of our departure on our family and psychically clear it with them. If they refuse, however, and if we want to please them, we may create a deep conflict about leaving and express that by "hanging on" physically by never quite healing or by going in and out of comas. Changing our mind about proceeding with this

Lifetime is also what occurs in crib-deaths, still-births and miscarriages.

Another reason for leaving this Lifetime as a child is not because the Lifetime was a mistake, but because it was a success. The entity achieved his desired experience and chose to depart. Not all successful Lifetimes have to be one hundred years long. As mentioned, some children can inspire more love and growth by the time they are five than many who have had the opportunity for decades, but chose instead to pollute with self-pity, violence and put downs. To leave a Lifetime early may be, for that person, the wisest choice available.

Many of us who have lost our children have experienced hell. And many of us who are losing or will lose our children will feel similarly hurt. I would like to offer a few suggestions in hopes we will make our process easier.

First, please realize that Life is not unjust. It may be unfair, but it is always just; all of us get exactly what we consciously or unconsciously want, all the time. Life is not cruel. Life is in no way interested in torturing our child or us. Life loves us.

Secondly, please feel all of our feelings about our loss, including anger at Life and God. Go ahead, even if we know those ideas are not accurate; if we feel it, express it, with harm to none. At this point, we might read helpful books about grieving or see a loving therapist to assist us in dealing with our feelings. But, please, let us not repress our emotions. Please give ourselves the gifts of our compassion and love; be loyal to our selves. Thirdly, after we have blown our emotional jets a while, please do not stay there and make ourselves a victim. Remember that all death is self-selected and Life is not attacking us. Do not fear, we will see and play with our child again - - love relationships definitely continue beyond the physical plane. We can see our child again while we are still here, but certainly more so after we close our Lifetime. It seems to me our job now is to get on with our Lives. Take what we have learned and expand into it; discover more of our true selves, set meaningful goals, work toward our destiny and imbue each moment of our awareness with as much love, gratitude and joy as we can. Become more involved with others and love them as we loved our child, or even more.

Next, a difficult idea, but so important to consider: please realize we set up our reality so that we could experience the struggle with disease or injury and the loss we have. We did not do this accidentally, but with purpose. Why, you ask? Well, I can guess at three possible motives, some of which may be difficult to accept, but nonetheless may contain some truth for us. One, to serve as a framework for our further growth (this is the most common motive). Two, to serve as another facet of our victim stance in Life. Or, three, to serve as a self-selected punishment. These last two motives are not particularly attractive, but most necessary to inspect and evaluate. Giving ourselves tragedies is a great habit to break. We can only do this, of course, with love and kindness to ourselves. Again, the assistance of a loving therapist can help us through these tumultuous times.

As unpleasant a possibility as this may be, if our children become ill, injured or die in the future, please keep these explanations in mind and refer to them as needed. At all times, focus as much as we can on our own love and compassion. Please realize that we have set up Earth experience so that everything and everyone is temporary, i.e. manifesting in time, with a beginning, middle and end. Let us do ourselves the favor of living in harmony with this truth; do not clutch at people or things and do not squander our current opportunities for joy. Be swift to love, make tracks to be kind.

GREAT PERMISSIONS

Whenever I had prospective parents, actual parents, or couples in therapy, I told them about four Great Permissions they would do well to give their kids and/or each other. Honestly giving these permissions releases ourselves from potential emotional hardship in the future. These permissions make our Lives easier because they are in more harmony with the truths of Life than what we are taught from our Paradigm One and Paradigm Two explanations of Life. These permissions do not mean we prefer the experiences described, but only that we do not mentally or emotionally fight them if they occur.

The four Great Permissions we would do well to give our loved ones are: 1) It is ok to be Gay, 2) It is ok to mess up your Life, 3) It is ok to die and

4) it's ok to leave me.

People *will* choose Gayness, *will* mess up their Lives, *will* die and *may* leave us! If we are not in harmony with these basic facts of Life, we can cause ourselves tons and tons of unnecessary misery and pain. "How *dare* you do *that* to me!" is a very old, worn, sad and unnecessary refrain sung throughout history by far too many of us because of our metaphysical ignorance that we each choose our own personal, subjective experience.

Some people do choose to be Gay. Some people do choose to mess up their Lives. All people choose to die. Many people leave others. Why fight it? Why hassle ourselves about their own, personal choices? Because we *own* them? Because we *must* have them ? No! They are free to be them as we are free to be us. Let us quit fighting Life and get on with the true business of why we are here: to learn how to become more loving and inclusive. Paradigm One and Paradigm Two, once helpful, are now making our Lives more difficult than they need to be. Ignorance of metaphysics is a heavy burden, one not to be taken lightly.

RECURRENCES

Once we heal a serious disease condition or put it into remission, the next most dreaded experience is a recurrence of that condition. This is especially true for cancer. Recurrence is actually a re-requisitioning of the original condition. I am aware of seven basic reasons for re-creating a disease condition. The first has to do with somatically informing ourselves that the belief and emotional blockages originally symbolized by the disease have not yet been released. A recurrence can be like a whistle signaling the psychological workers back to the job of emotional resolution.

The second reason I am aware of for re-activating a disease condition has to do with fear of letting the problem go. What would we be so afraid of, you might ask, that we would actually prefer to re-create something as severe as cancer? Well, there are several facets to this answer. Many of us keep our problems around simply because they are so familiar to us - - well traveled psychic territory that has a predictable, martyrish feel to it and a meager, but familiar, set of payoffs (payoffs are hidden emotional goals we have which motivate the requisition of negative events. Some common payoffs are: self-pity (the big one!), punishment of self or other, keeping ourselves down because of guilt, seeking negative attention or manipulating others or ourselves).

And some of us are so very sure that Life must be filled with problems or else we would not feel alive. So we unconsciously prefer to be half-alive battling problems than "un-alive", free of distress.

The next fear of letting a problem go is a big one: some of us, unfortunately, are simply so used to having and battling difficulties that we have built struggle into our self-concept and identity. To let go of a problem would be to not be true to our (old) selves and old self-image. It is vitally important that we learn everything we can about the topic of self-image and, over the course of our whole Lifetime, continually revise and polish-up our set of self-defining beliefs and attitudes.

Fourthly, we may allow our self to heal and later bring back the negative condition as a way of giving ourselves a few more rounds in the ring with melodramatic struggle and suffering. It is a way of reclaiming our victim status and a way of showing the world just how very, very difficult our Life is; it is a way of continuing to live as the melodramatic underdog. And here is a very important point: choosing struggle and suffering can also be a way of manipulating others or Goddess-God to take care of us and provide for us (they won't). Fifthly, recurrences can be chosen because many of us are afraid of our creativity, power and success. Thus, disease problems become a convenient excuse or *hiding place* to avoid the scary, successful powerful parts of ourselves and our futures.

Sixth, some of us would just love to succeed and have fun and are not afraid of doing so, but believe in guilt and saddle ourselves with it and may unconsciously choose a recurrence of a health problem to hold ourselves back and/or punish ourselves until we somehow "become better" and *earn* the "reward" of a happy Life.

A different guilt that could motivate a re-requisitioned recurrence is a symbiotic guilt. As described in Chapter Three, this is a very common agreement we make with loved ones in which we promise to hold ourselves back from success and fun until they can have it, too. We, in effect, retard our emotional progress until they catch up. This guilt contract is born out of our caring for them and our desire to be connected, but provides the obvious self-defeating effect of us denying ourselves increased levels of choice, love, success and fun. Good to research it and if we find this ugly guilt, release it and allow others to live as they prefer and find other ways to be close.

The final reason I am aware of for choosing a recurrence of a Lifetime- threatening disease is because of a wavering in our desire between continuing this Lifetime or ending it. We may bring the disease condition back to have a way out available, tucked in our back pocket, as it were, in case we want to utilize it as an exit route later.

Recurrences can be very frightening to us and our family and must be dealt with honestly and compassionately. The issues of martyrish melodrama, fear of letting the disease go, incomplete releasing of toxic belief and emotion, guilt and, especially, whether we really want to stick around and *why* or why not are very important to explore. Again, because these issues usually involve more than one person, they indicate the importance and value of family therapy. I sincerely wish everyone who is dealing with the issue of recurrence a whole lot of your own love, compassion, honesty and power as you work to make wise choices for yourselves

OTHER DISEASES

Let us now take a quick look at the dynamics behind some other common and not so common disease conditions. I realize that dealing with metaphysical ideas, their attendant responsibilities and the emotional impacts thereof will take great courage for many of us. I believe we all have that courage and power within us and I hope we will nurture ourselves enough to tap into and use ours (thankfully, we can ask our Higher Selves for help). I write with much compassion for our feelings as we deal with ourselves and our conditions. I have had my hard times dealing with responsibility and anger for creating problems, too, so I can empathize with how difficult this probably is for some of us, especially having it come at us all at once as it is in this book. Hang in there! We are very strong and the true self will help us, as we desire.

I will now describe some emotional dynamics which may be going on in us; please evaluate them and see if they fit. The dynamics described may not fit us and, if not, please explore further to find those that do.

"STOP THE WORLD DISORDERS"

These are physical disorders which, through discussions with Lazaris, I was rather surprised to learn about. These conditions are designed to really put the brakes on in our Life.

The following discussion may seem to some to rationalize people's failures or to coddle and excuse weakness. After all, some people have it "tough" in Life and they make it! Why can't we all be tough; after all, we need to survive! Sure. I want to remind you that we are not all alike, that our emotional Life is paramount in Human nature and that we range on a sensitivity continuum from numb to highly aware (remember our comparison of a crayfish and a Human, mentioned in Chapter Three?). Thus, what feels like a pinch to some may be a snake bite to others. The most sensitive people feel the impacts of events deeper and more intensely than those who are just skating along on the emotional surface. Again, everything is subjective. Please read the following dynamics with an open mind and a compassionate heart; and please lose any judgments.

When we are children, we all want to receive safety, love and security from our caretakers on whom we greatly rely. These are the emotional nutrients of childhood, of which we all have minimum daily requirements. When we do not get the nurturing we want, some of us, in effect, emotionally sit down, cross our arms, scowl and determinedly say: "Hey, I am getting gypped! This sucks! Well, I am not budging from this spot until Mommy or Daddy gives me my love. I want my love!" Our daily world and body physically progress in time; emotionally, however, we are still sitting there, stuck at age five or so, waiting (please remember: there is no time in the realm of emotion). Later on, we may not want to enter adolescence because we did not get the love we wanted at five and we are sure as hell we will not get it at fifteen; plus we have all the "burdens" of adulthood soon coming down upon us after that. So, many of us emotionally dig in further and stop, but again our body keeps going. It secretes new hormones and matures physically quite on its own, carrying us along, Our Child Within screaming and kicking all the while. This is the panic of adolescence: we are not filled up as children, we become teens without a clue what to be now, although we think we know it all, often using "better than" as a refuge. Soon we have to face becoming responsible for ourselves and making a living by carving a niche for ourselves in a masculine-energy-dominated society that really does not care one damn bit about how we feel, just as long as we look good and produce. This is the circumstance many chronological adults find ourselves in - - physically mature, but rather stuck, living as an emotional child or adolescent still dealing with the same fear-based issues. We can cause ourselves great struggle and even trauma coping with daily Life when we have not matured emotionally. And this difficulty can be exacerbated because our society is still in its adolescent stage of emotional development.

This is the great growth issue for our near future - - to work to mature into emotional adulthood, both individually and societally. This is The New Age; a wonderful period of first-time-available, wide spread emotional maturity. This is the root requirement of spiritual, bodily and financial winnerhood: to consciously decide to view and live our reality from a mature, adult perspective; one based on spiritual values and approaches of love, responsibility, honesty, authenticity, trust, receiving, acting with harm to none and integrity.

As far as Stopping The World disorders go: as the river of Life and time flow through us, some of us may not want to flow with it and therefore create disturbances which seek to, in effect, stop motion. I would like to discuss six such conditions: Autism, Multiple Sclerosis, Muscular Dystrophy, Parkinson's, Huntington's Chorea and Alzheimer's Disease.

AUTISM

I won't describe the many symptoms of Autism except to say that it is often called childhood schizophrenia. Autism is an inner choice a child makes in which he says: "No way. Uh-uh! I am not going to grow up. I am staying right here, right here at age one and a half. Screw you!" A child may choose this condition because of a paralyzing fear to move into more complicated developmental tasks or because he feels he made a wrong choice for this Lifetime, but does not want to die again and, in effect, mentally suspends himself between two worlds. Autism can also be chosen as a Lifetime framework in which to explore free, unbridled emotion; unlike previous Lifetimes in which "controlled" (i.e. deadened) facades were chosen.

The degree of self-selection in Autism is fairly apparent. When we explore some of the diseases that we will discuss next, however, it can become more difficult for people to accept responsibility for creating them. I think if I had some of these conditions and I was learning this view of my disease condition and metaphysics for the first time, I would likely have trouble accepting them - - even get angry at the suggestion that I gave myself such intense problems. My family might feel the same; as if I am suggesting the ill person was a hypochondriac or something.

Well, I am not implying such; I can well empathize with the difficulty of accepting the ultra-responsibility metaphysics suggests. Sometimes it is hard to know the truth and deal with it. Without the truth, however, we lose our personal power. Without our personal power, we shun our gifts to create. Without our choice to create, we can settle and just accept our "Fate" and can easily give in to our Negative Ego's games of victimhood and martyrhood. With the concomitant self-pity, we lose touch with our Higher Selves, our Souls and Goddess-God. That greatly sucks. Better to have the discomfort of responsibility than the powerlessness of ignorance and denial. So, with much courage we continue.

MUSCULAR DYSTROPHY (MD) AND MULTIPLE SCLEROSIS (MS)

In each disease the dominant feature is muscle impairment; uncontrolled movements, spasticity and/or degeneration. I know of four motives involved in choosing these conditions. One motive is a common one for severe conditions: to have the disease serve as a framework of growth, an experiential mountain to triumphantly climb over (which a lot of people do).

A second motive is to stop our world; to slow, slow, slow down movement (symbolized by muscle) in our Life. In MD, we try to slow down in childhood and in MS we try to stop our seemingly crazy, hurtful world in early adulthood (usually 20 to 40 years of age). Also, Muscular Dystrophy is a hereditary disease, usually indicating a desire to please a parent, that side of the family or what they represent. We want to slow down our world so we can get an emotional grip on it. For instance, many of us have attracted events in which we feel overwhelmed, inept, powerless, picked-on and bounced around. Too many of these hurtful experiences can lead to broken dreams and a desire to quit and hide from the seemingly cruel world. MD or MS can dramatically slow our pace of interaction with our hurtful world and provide much needed respite from expected cruelties or failures.

A third motive for selecting either of these conditions has to do with our self-image. We may build into our identity a belief that we are a psychically or physically weak person. We usually do not like this belief and attendant thoughts because they generate feelings of helplessness. Thus, we understandably *try* to gloss over and deny them away (please remember: once an emotion is created, it cannot be denied away; it can only be repressed out of awareness. It has to be felt away.). Well, at some later time we may choose to confront our self-image and experience a body condition in which we become physically weak to reflect the emotional view we have of ourselves (surprisingly, this can be exacerbated by self-images from other Lifetimes. Please remember - - there is not time in the realm of emotion). These physical conditions provide the opportunity to rail against and overcome our weak self-perception. This motive seems to pertain more to MS because we have had more of an opportunity to deny our beliefs and feelings of weakness and thus have more of a need to confront ourselves.

A fourth motive for creating MD or MS is to create a framework in which to overcome a fear. We may have a tremendous fear of being physically weak and dependent. Thus, we may, with great courage or extremism, force a total confrontation with our unconscious emotions by living and facing our feared dependence brought about through muscle impairment.

I imagine these are difficult ideas for some of us to cope with. But only through responsibility and love can we heal in our heart and body - - I wish us the very best of our true selves as we deal with our growth issues; the purpose of this book is to assist us in that.

PARKINSON'S DISEASE

We usually develop Parkinson's Disease late in Life. There is a gradual deterioration of the brain, which causes difficulty with muscular movements, including characteristic tremors of the hands and head. As with many diseases (cancer, MS, colitis, etc.), medical science does not yet know the physical cause of Parkinson's Disease. The medical establishment almost always talks about brain chemicals and genes. Brain chemicals (hormones, enzymes, oxidants, free-radicals, etc.) and genetics, however, are the result of inner choices to manipulate the body to produce a desired physical condition.

Basically what is happening emotionally in the person with Parkinson's is that we have been feeling burdened in our Lives and feel we cannot take it anymore. We reflect our emotions in our symptoms; we lose our balance easily, our back and shoulders become burdenly bent forward and our gait very restricted (low aggression shuffle). We feel intense burdens of not enough power, too much responsibility, too much pressure, too much to do and too much to think. So much so, we unconsciously slow down our brain which generates all these activities. We can also begin an autonomic, repetitive side to side tremble in our head, as if we are shaking our head to say over and over to the world: "No, no, no".

Another factor in creating Parkinson's Disease has to do with common, limiting ideas about old age. Some people believe the rubbish that as our body gets older we will "naturally" deteriorate; our eyes will weaken, our ears will go deaf, our back will hurt a lot, our joints will calcify and our sex desires will evaporate. Well, most unfortunately some people think that when they get to a certain age they will get a debilitating disease like Parkinson's; and they do.

Finally, we may choose a disease like Parkinson's because we want to begin our preparation to die, much as when an airplane first begins its descent to land. Through Parkinson's Disease and others like it, we can taper off our Earthly involvements slowly, gradually withdrawing and withdrawing, until we make a smooth, soft landing on the other side.

HUNTINGTON'S CHOREA

This disease is similar to the previous ones in that it is "caused" by a degeneration of our brain and is accompanied by loss of muscle control. Our movements become involuntarily and continually spastic. The severity of this condition can progress to unpleasant personality changes and even dementia. Huntington's Chorea is a hereditary disease and is therefore involved with a person's loyalty to a parent or side of the family. Along with loyalty, Huntington's Chorea seems to involve a deep insecurity about self. The person's thinking before he began his Lifetime likely went something like: "If I can be just like mom or dad or their families, then maybe I will be good enough and they will love me. I have to imitate them and play up to them; it is the only way I can get love, 'cause I am really a nothing person." Thus, the spastic, shaking movements of the body reflect a shakiness in the person's emotional reality; feeling shaky about getting love based on the assumed poor quality of one's own worth and love.

ALZHEIMER'S DISEASE

This is a disorder previously referred to as senility; it is very similar to Parkinson's and Huntington's. The symptoms of severe loss of concentration, memory, reason, interest, coherent speech and bodily control are the bases of this condition. Alzheimer's Disease generally follows the dynamics of Parkinson's Disease. I think many of us contract for this disease when we are in our 50s, the time when our Soul asks us if we want to progress into wisdom or fade into avoidance (more on this in the section about prostate problems). Not wanting to progress in our Life to our next set of growth challenges and maturity, usually because of the interplay of deprivation, fear, ignorance, weak self-image and repressed rage, a person inwardly selects to stop psychic growth and reverses same to bygone days of childhood yore.

As someone who worked as a psychotherapist, I have had several people say to me that they would like to die. And then some people have said there have been times in their Lives they felt so emotionally burdened they would have just loved to take a pill and go into a coma for a few years. And I well remember a client who told me the happiest time of her Life was when she was four years old. After that, everything changed - - her parents fought more, they were emotionally aloof, she had to go to school; her world became darker from an increase of pressure and a lack of love. My client told me she really wished she could be four again; she thought about it often. She was thirty six when she told me this.

What is happening for these people, is a desire to stop movement into further (assumed) emotional pain. If this woman who longs to be four again (because that is when she felt the happiest) does not resolve her conflicts and emotions, and keeps going on her present course, then it is easy to imagine that when she turns sixty five, she might stop everything and go backward to live forever in Happy Land, which is all she ever wanted, all any of us really want - - to feel secure, loved, cherished and to just be our true selves.

The beautiful part of her story is that we worked therapeutically so she could heal her emotional wounds of the past and progress into her own security, love and dignity, thus releasing the pull her earliest years had for her. This healing is available to anyone who wants it - - to aggress forth in our Lives in love, power, meaning, success and tons of silly, exhilarating fun. All we have to do is want to and then *learn how* to do it.

A final motive in selecting a Stop The World disorder involves a very dignified and beautiful experience that becomes rather distorted. Each of us, you see, has a deep inner need, as Lazaris puts it, to "go home". This means we have a desire to emotionally unite with the higher aspects of our being: our Higher Self and Soul. Our desire to "go home" is our longing for the spiritual fulfillment of conscious self-completion. We can, of course, achieve this auto-merger to wonderfully satisfying degrees through meditation, conscious dream work and astral projection. Some of us, however, who do not know about our Souls, Higher Selves or meditation and yet intently yearn for the deepest connection with self, think going home is to be found in our childhoods, the developmental home of this Lifetime. Thus, we regress to our third birthday party and stay there hoping that will satisfy our homeward spiritual pull, which it will not.

Concerning treating Stop The World conditions, I recommend working psychically at first, then apply the standard treatments. Loving, telepathic contacts can serve nicely as an initial bridge from one person's world to another's. Let us talk to the afflicted person mentally while we touch him. Love him. As difficult as it may be for us to do, give him permission to choose what he has chosen, knowing he either made a wise choice or a mistake. If it is too difficult for us to do this, then back off until we can. Then psychically encourage him to explore alternative ways in dealing with his feelings. Tell him it is ok to hate, ok to feel weak, ok to succeed, ok to like himself (importantly, help him distinguish inner worth from outer worth) and that it is ok for him to ask for your help (if you really want to give it, that is), or seek help from a loving therapist. Conscious telepathic communication is an important aspect of future healing, education and who knows what else? Let it come from our love.

DIABETES

Diabetes is one of the most pernicious diseases Humans have. It is an ugly condition that sets off several syndromes which can result in rabid destruction of our body.

Insulin is a hormone secreted by the pancreas that is needed to escort sugar from our blood into our body's cells. Our cells then happily dine on this beautiful sugar (glucose) and produce energy so we can live and function. When our cells do not get this much, much needed sugar, they starve. They really do not like this and they rebel. They do this by slowing down; some even die. This leads to a myriad of other physical problems such as: neuropathy (dying nerves), retinopathy (the retina dies and we go blind), heart problems, circulatory problems, amputations and kidney failure; these conditions are symbolic in and of themselves.

There are two onsets of diabetes: when we are young (even when born) and when we are older. Young people create diabetes for different reasons than older people, usually for the ol' standby of a framework for this Lifetime or to symbolize issues they brought with them from another Lifetime. Older people usually create diabetes to symbolize issues they have not resolved in this Lifetime.

Diabetes, whether caused by cell malfunction or insulin deficiency, is a condition in which glucose stays in our blood and does not enter our hungry cells to nourish them. This reflects a great deal of frustration and anger that we are feeling. We symbolize through our body that we are mad as hell that Life has not treated us "sweet" enough. The much anticipated sweetness of Life, which we feel was denied to us, is therefore denied to our cells. The nourishment of glucose stays in our blood and gets us nowhere. We, and our cells, want our sweetness !!!

To work to resolve these issues, we would do well to hunt out our frustrations and repressed angers. We then need to feel them, release them With Harm To None. We would also do well to check out herbs and natural approaches to balancing our blood sugar.

Young people would do well to ask their parents to help them find a reputable past-Life therapist who can help them discover the old reasons why they brought the disease into this Lifetime. If early onset diabetes is being used as a framework for this Lifetime, however, it may not be too amenable to change; unless a new decision is powerfully made (which can happen).

EPILEPSY

Epilepsy is a nervous disorder in which our brain impulses are disrupted so that seizures and even convulsions result. There are two types of epilepsy, Petit Mal and Grand Mal. Petit Mal epilepsy involves seizure, but minimal convulsions and usually occurs in children who often outgrow (release) the condition by their early twenties. In Grand Mal epilepsy, however, convulsions can occur that are thrashingly severe, sometimes leading to loss of consciousness.

The basic dynamic involved in epilepsy is that of an emotional circuit breaker, as when the body goes into shock. The person's perception is blanked out because of an emotional overload, a strong desire to not perceive anymore and to escape. Muscles are twitched and convulsed to "shake off" the pressures from unpleasant, even intolerable, aspects of our Lives (including those exacerbated by the epilepsy). These unpleasant aspects could include a poor self-image, severe pain and rage from emotional abuse, lack of love, domination, strong fears, perfectionism, anxiety or the accumulation of each of these.

AUTO-IMMUNE DISORDERS

Auto-immune disorders are diseases in which our body's immune system turns on our body and attacks our own tissues. This happens in conditions like myasthenia gravis, rheumatoid arthritis, lupus erythematosus, pernicious anemia, thyroiditis, rheumatic fever and others. The emotional mechanism which makes our body's immune mechanism turn on itself is a desire to burden or hurt ourselves, usually because of disliking ourselves. Along with disliking ourselves, we usually create concomitant pockets of disappointment, anger and/or guilt. It is as if we are beating ourselves up in slow motion by chipping away at our joints, muscles, lymph, blood or heart.

Therapy would ideally focus on taking responsibility for the disease, discovering the negative self-image and any feelings of self-hate, guilt and punishment, evaluating reasons for the feelings (including anger at someone else turned upon ourselves), releasing them, changing negative beliefs, forgiving others and then forgiving ourselves.

ANOREXIA NERVOSA

Anorexia Nervosa is a disorder usually chosen by adolescent girls, but one that can be chosen by adolescent boys and sometimes adults. It is a condition in which the person obsesses about not getting fat. Food becomes the enemy. In order to not have a fat body, the person compulsively undereats and over exercises, often into a state of malnutrition and, if unchecked, often into organ damage and eventual starvation.

Recently, many more females than ever before have tried anorexia and bulimia, as eating disorders have increased to an alarming degree since the '80s. The more common type of anorexia usually is not Anorexia Nervosa - - I call it "Anorexia Populara."

It seems to be related to our fashion, cosmetics and advertising industries, merged with inferiority on the part of many adolescent females as they seek to "fit in", be sexily popular and even be "better than" the unpopular females. It most often is a symptom of a girl's painful confusion of her inner worth with outer worth, i.e. if she is thin enough, maybe she will be pretty enough, sexy enough, universally desired and then she will be ok (maybe).

Interesting to note: a study conducted by the American Association of University Women in 1991 found that 60 percent of the sample of girls in elementary school were satisfied with themselves. In high school, the figure dropped to 29 percent. [6] Likely, this is when the girls' inner worth-outer worth confusion collided with our culture's sexism and cosmetic programming.

Many girls cannot live up to the carefully crafted, unrealistic image they are taught they ought to. So they "fail". Females are taught to make up for being female; they can best do this by being attractive to men, according to the standards set by men and a male-dominated culture.

All of this is most tragic because the self-rejection and starvation of Anorexia Populara are incredibly unnecessary and so painful. These could be easily avoided if only girls had been taught when two years old that their inner worth is inherent. Then they would not have made their outer-worth-popularity into such a sacrifice-demanding-god. Unfortunately, a similar distortion happens to males; usually not to compete to see who can be thinner and prettier, but often to see who can be more macho and more violent (pass the steroids, please). Both are perverse.

Anorexia Nervosa preceded Anorexia Populara by many years. Anorexia Nervosa is a serious condition and a sad one to watch occur. Basically what is happening is that the person feels absolutely terrible emotionally, usually feeling intense loneliness, sadness, fear and rage. These people usually feel a lot of self-hate. They often feel heavily dominated and suppressed (their domination, usually by their parents, may be actual or imagined; most often actual). They also tend to think they are low-Lifes, not deserving of much, not even to nourish themselves.

Anorexic people cope with their wracking unhappiness by choosing to waste away, to die. It is their way out of the pain from tremendous self-rejection. It is also their last stand on the holy ground of self-determination: "You can't push me around anymore. I will not take it! You cannot shove things down my throat anymore. You cannot even make me eat. You can't even make me live! Screw you! Now I will decide! It is the only control I have and I'm going to keep it. Just try! Go ahead, just *try* to make me live. You can't! Besides, I don't even know if I deserve to live." The anorexic person is in intense emotional pain and rage and needs to release these. They also need love (nourishment), the kind with no strings attached, and lots of it (Anorexia Populara people, too), especially from themselves.

With adolescent girls, their menstrual periods stop after a while of not eating. Thus, they achieve in a fashion their strong desire to "roll back the clock" to the Halcyon days of being a child, where there likely was more innocence, more of a feeling of worth and less hurt. For adults who choose this condition, they are likely trying to shrink their bodies with hopes their responsibilities, pressures and anxieties will also shrink.

VARICOSE VEINS

Varicose veins is a condition in which we do not allow our veins, usually in our lower legs, to function adequately. Valves in our veins are told to break down and then blood collects in stagnant pools, bulging the veins out so they look like swollen, knotty cords just under our skin. Varicose veins can be a very painful condition.

Basically what is happening is that we are communicating to ourselves that we are having trouble standing up for ourselves and are feeling unsupported (leg concerns), particularly by our family (blood concerns). We feel angry about this lack of support, so much that so our leg looks like it is going to burst at the seams.

PSORIASIS

Psoriasis is a chronic skin disease in which scaly red patches appear on our body, primarily on our elbows and knees.

Unfortunately, there is no medical cure for "the heartbreak of psoriasis", so many of us suffer from the discomfort and unsightliness of the lesions for a long time. Of course, there is a cure and it has to do with working through the emotional communications we are giving ourselves.

Since the skin represents our self-image and elbows are joints (flexibility) that are third chakra ruled, regarding emotional expression, and knees are second chakra ruled, regarding sensual pleasure, the condition of psoriasis indicates a conflict over these four. That is, we indicate we have an image of ourselves which is rigidly anti-emotional and anti-pleasure and we do not like it anymore and feel angry about it. We may have been taught to think of ourselves as being ok because we are strict, prim and proper. Certainly not silly (so sad). With this sober stiffness we rigidly rob ourselves of our Lives' pleasures and personal, little joys. Thus we attack our suffocating self-image (our skin) and communicate our anger and intense longing for sensual pleasure, silly spontaneity and the healing balm of emotional freedom for our beautiful Child Within.

PROSTATE PROBLEMS

The prostate gland helps produce and store seminal fluid. It is an important part of the male reproductive system and, since it is located in the male's genital area, it is second chakra ruled. It is also located close to our first chakra area and indicates concerns about security as well. Thus, problems in the prostate gland indicate issues (most often anger and fear) about a lack of pleasure and creativity and a growing insecurity, most often tied into how one is living the male role.

In order to understand "the male role", one needs to understand the current focus of our culture. As mentioned, our mass mind set has been that of a distorted masculine energy approach. We have all labored under standards that resemble a Conquistador mind set. We all have been conquered and warped because our society prefers domination, comparison, competition, appearance, order, structure, obligation, duty, performance and logic to the exclusion of feminine energy attributes. Our societal customs do not allow much "room" for deep pleasure, sensitivity or creativity. The feminine energy values of love, spirituality, imagination, creativity, togetherness, cooperation, receiving, passion, support and Soul are mostly allowed in songs or movies, not corporate Life. Sadly, often not even in family Life.

Thus, prostate problems serve as convenient indicators that the man is having a large amount of difficulty finding and living his pleasure and spirituality (the highest pleasure of all).

Prostate problems usually do not occur until a man hits his 40s or 50s. That is because of two basic reasons. One, because we Humans are so powerful, we can adapt to a lot of struggle and store up a lot of repressed emotion before we show signs of distress. By the time a fellow is in his 40s or 50s, he may have filled his emotion-storage tanks with so much anger he wishes to communicate that he has finally reached maximum levels allowed.

The second reason many men will wait until their 50s to communicate their pleasure problems is because the 50s are a special time of Life in all people. It is one of the most important phases in our Soul's growth - - a time of reflection on the quality of Life we have lived. During the mid 50s, according to Lazaris, we inwardly assess our Lives and determine if we want to creatively proceed in wisdom or if we want to chuck it all and regress. Remember our discussion about Alzheimer's Disease? Often it is in the mid 50s when people make the decision to regress and, in effect, submit their inner requisition for Alzheimer's.

Often men will signal their insecurity and anger about lack of pleasure by using prostate problems in their 50s because they really do want to progress to their next stage of Life in wisdom, but have not been allowing themselves enough pleasure thus far to make the jump (mid-Life crisis). They are signaling they have a lot of catching-up to do; they can certainly do this, once they contact their Child Within and honor his wishes about what is really fun for him; not some stupid, societally-suggested, parentally approved "role". An enlarged prostate indicates a swelling anger; cancer in the prostate indicates anger that is exploding.

MENSTRUAL DIFFICULTIES

This is a bit of a loaded topic to write about because of the many sexist attitudes toward women and their menstrual process. Through the years, menstruation has been used by sexist men and women to bolster their arguments that women are by nature emotionally unstable. It is with much pleasure that I write this section to challenge those stereotypes by describing some emotional dynamics responsible for menstrual difficulties.

I think it important to state first off that because men do not menstruate, some men think they are better than women. Men certainly do have bodily cycles and even experience menopause, too, but to a lesser degree. If men did have menstrual cycles, we would likely have any and all of the menstrual difficulties women do, perhaps even more. With that acknowledged, let us proceed. Many women, of course, do not experience any emotional or physical difficulties before or during their menstrual cycles. They have no symptoms to restrict activities or severely affect their moods. Indeed, no woman has to experience menstrual difficulties.

Millions of women do, however, experience difficult times either before or during their monthly cycle. There is a growing awareness and effort being made to assist women who experience Pre-Menstrual Syndrome (PMS), an unpleasant cluster of symptoms that usually begins two weeks before the woman's cycle. The physical causes of PMS are not yet determined, though a hormonal imbalance (progesterone) is highly suspected. Several organizations are set up to support women with PMS, to assure them they are not "crazy" and that there is a physical root to their physical and emotional swings.

The roots of PMS and any other menstrual difficulty are, metaphysically speaking, located in one's beliefs and emotions; they create the hormonal imbalances and other physical problems. Again, let us watch out for people who may try to use this information to strengthen and justify their anti-female attitudes. They may run the old tape that says women are more emotionally upset than men. Therefore, society cannot trust women to be rational, dependable and "strong" and therefore women are inferior to men, but ok for having babies, keeping kitchens clean and being sex objects.

Though the first premise of this line of thinking is valid, the conclusion is not. Women may indeed be more emotionally upset (i.e. hurt and angry) than men. With the centuries of psychological abuse women have had heaped on them, they have very good reasons to be emotionally upset. To use a normal Human reaction as a "proof" of physical or emotional "inferiority", however, is absurd; it is the result of a heavy fear and an immature handling of that fear.

So, as I discuss the belief and emotional factors behind menstrual difficulties, please realize that these concerns are temporary, once a woman becomes aware of them and works to process out her emotion and change her beliefs. When a body message is understood and correctively acted on, any person can remove the previously needed symptoms. Women who are giving themselves menstrual difficulties can stop doing that and breeze through a period without any hassle whatsoever. In this regard, menstrual difficulties are just like any other bodily disturbance and in no way indicate lack of worth, ability or competence.

A suggestion: it is always wise to medically evaluate and appropriately treat all physical factors that may be affecting us, such as hormone levels or allergies. So, with that stated, let us now inspect six emotional factors for women with problematic periods to consider.

The first area to inspect, of course, is a woman's general emotional state. As you know, in menses a woman's body releases tissues it does not need anymore; obviously to retain the tissue would be damaging to her health. Along with the physical toxicity, emotional toxicity is also sloughed off; the two piggyback during a menstrual cycle. Therefore, if a woman is experiencing, or has repressed, a lot of frustration, sadness, fear, guilt and/or anger, she will also release these during menses and she will likely experience more emotional swings and physical discomfort. It would therefore be wise for her to inspect, evaluate and work through her feelings as she creates them, so there would not be as much emotional "stuff" stored in her system trying to be released once a month. I want to point out here that men also release emotional build-ups from our systems, but we do not have a menstrual process to piggyback on. We are likely to choose other body parts, cars, electronics or our work to reflectively communicate through.

A second emotional factor to consider is that of "secondary gains", i.e. receiving emotional payoffs from problematic periods. The usual ones are: attention, lessened responsibilities, pity, domination and approval. I suggest women evaluate their possible participation with each of these, find other ways to get their needs met (i.e. honestly loving and asserting themselves) and release their physical discomfort. Meditation and auto suggestion can work well.

A third factor that may be operative is a belief that such difficulties natural and to be expected. This could also tie into a secondary gain of winning approval and expressing loyalty. If women who are important to a young girl are experiencing moderate to harsh symptoms during their periods, it becomes very easy to internalize and manifest these symptoms as a means of belonging to the group. That group might be her mother, sisters, friends, or Womankind in general. Here are three good questions to ask oneself: would it really be ok with them if you had symptom-free periods? Would it be ok with you if you had symptom-free periods? Would it be ok with you if it was not ok with them if you had symptom-free periods?

A fourth emotional factor for women to inspect is their beliefs and feelings about being a female this Lifetime (that is a idiom: actually she cannot *be* a female, nor can a male *be* a male. Our bodies are visceral robes we are wearing, not *what* or *who* we truly are. We are spirits.).

You see, if a little girl is taught by her parents or her culture that being a female is somehow "less than" being a male (sadly, this lie is still policy in far too many countries), she will likely internalize this damaging superstition and use it against herself to dislike her Femaleness and her self. As mentioned earlier, emotional difficulties about our sex are usually symbolized through our reproductive system. Thus, if being a female is not ok with her and if Femaleness is defined in part by having menstrual cycles, then she may make her periods painful to symbolize her painful displeasure at being (oppressed as a) female.

A fifth motive to consider in analyzing problematic periods is one's beliefs and feelings about growing up. One day she's a child and the next day her menses begins and she is catapulted across the developmental line into fertile adolescence. As we have discussed in the Stop The World disorders, if a girl is not ready to let go of her childhood, particularly if she has not yet received the security, love and validation she wants, she may fiercely resist her adolescence and the bloody intrusive process her body is forcing upon her. Physical maturation can be absolutely traumatic for some girls and is not to be taken lightly.

A sixth motive for giving oneself problematic periods has to do with guilt and punishment. Because menses involves the release of blood, family concerns could be operative. Thus, it is important to inspect guilt and punishment relative to relatives.

I once had a client whom I will call Darlene, which is not her actual name. Darlene, like an increasing number of women, gave up custody of her children when her husband divorced her. For her, this was a smart, but very difficult decision to make. A little while after that, Darlene had her fallopian tubes tied. Then she began to experience severe distress during menses - - clotting a lot and experiencing much pain. As we analyzed the messages resident in her condition, it became apparent that Darlene's clotting was a thickening of concern about her family - - guilt about leaving her kids and possibly betraying cultural (and her mother's) expectations that she have more children. Darlene then set about to release those limited definitions of Womanhood, transmuting her guilt, expressing anger at being oppressed into a stereotypic role and then worked to forgive herself for beating herself up for not matching cultural standards and not loving herself enough in the first place to earlier redefine those standards. Thankfully, Darlene is doing well now.

For women who can identify with the above three paragraphs, I suggest you inspect your early beliefs and feelings about being a female and about growing up and replace them with more healthful ones. A *great* and very powerful way to do this is to meditate and imagine yourself as a little girl the hour before you started to believe the harmful ideas about being a female or an hour before you started your period. Go visit her. Introduce your current self to that girl and have a gentle talk with her. Ask her how she feels. In the situation of not being prepared for your period, explain to your little girl what is about to happen before it happens. Find out how she feels about it and help her express any fears, angers and sorrows (use the same process for not liking being a female). This process will most likely take several or many visits. Then discuss with that little girl the beauty and dignity of her Lifetime, her sex and her body. Help her believe in herself. The important point is that someone who cares about her is there for her and that she gets to blow off some emotional steam about her Life and what is happening to her. This is a very loving and therefore powerful method of taking care of oneself, of healing oneself. I hope you will avail yourself of it, using common sense and compassion as you proceed. Realize this: you can help your little girl grow up better than you did. What a beautiful idea! What a great, loving gift to give her. And only *you* can give it to her because she lives in your mind and only you can reach her through your imagination and emotion. Of course, this meditative method works equally for men who need to work with their little boys.

CATARACTS

A cataract is a condition in which the normally clear lens of our eye becomes cloudy. Vision through an eye may be diminished, blurred, doubled or totally blocked out. We create a cataract in our eye to signal that we have much difficulty seeing the truth. This difficulty could arise because of fear, anger or too much Negative Ego. As far as fear is concerned, the left or right eye indicates which of our energies (feminine or masculine) or which sex we find scary to view and deal with. Also, we may prefer cherished illusions and feel afraid to see the truth of ourselves, world conditions or people around us. And, if we saw the truth, we may have to act on it and that might be very scary.

Another motive could be that we may feel so angry about being unfulfilled that we may not want to see the issues or relationships (male or female) around us. Also, an inflated Negative Ego always clouds perception of our true self and the truth of our interactions. The Negative Ego does this by suggesting we deny responsibility and our feelings by playing better than or worse than and by making suggestions that can only lead to self-pity; all of which, of course, serve to lose sight of our primary reality, love.

GLAUCOMA

Glaucoma is an unpleasant condition in which our eye's liquid unhealthfully collects in a tiny duct behind our eyeball. As this reservoir of fluid increases in size, it can put pressure on our eye, causing pain and disturbed vision. Basically what is happening is a collection of emotion. As noted in Chapter Three, in our Earth system water is symbolic of emotion. Water that flows out of our eyes, of course, is a tear which often indicates sadness. Therefore, an increasing pressure on our eyeball from an accumulation of fluid indicates a buildup of emotion, most often sadness. Also, we may not want to see and understand what is causing our sadness so we stockpile our emotion and purposely throw our vision out of whack. Right or left eye indicates the sex of the person(s) our sadness pertains to.

TINNITUS

Tinnitus is a condition in which we place a continual buzzing or ringing sound in one or both ears. It is chronic background noise that only we can hear; we usually do not like it, but have to adapt because it does not stop. We are denied the wonder and blissful beauty of silence. The physical excuses used to explain Tinnitus can be motorcycles, gun discharges, whip-lash, ampped-up rock concerts, loud industrial equipment, football fans or other decibel damagers. Truly, these sources of noise pollution can be toxic to a Human, but they are not the true cause.

Usually we will place a chronic buzzing in our ears because we do not want to hear quiet. We usually do this because we originally wanted to hear the sounds of love and acceptance, but instead heard rejection and hurt. Our ears love to register the truth of love and when they do not, we may want to create some interference so it is harder to receive the negativity. The unloving sounds we want to block out could be coming from people, society or from our own self-deprecating, punishing thoughts.

Also, we may be frightened to hear our other thoughts; frightened by our greed, repressed rage, arrogance or other unsavory qualities. We may also be frightened of meditating and going deeper into our core, feeling selves; so we crank-up our background noise to keep ourselves at a level of inner-avoidant-discomfort. Right or left ear gives a huge clue to decipher who we want to block out.

STROKES

A stroke is a very serious condition caused by either blocked blood supply to our brain or a bursting of blood vessels in our brain. A stroke can impair speech, movement and/or memory. We give ourselves strokes because of a welling up of pressure within ourselves. It is as if we have so much deprivation, disappointment, loneliness and anger repressed inside us that we cannot take it anymore and either shut down or burst. Also, we may feel as if we would like to blow up our whole reality and start over, but cannot, so we, in effect explode ourselves instead.

Strokes are often chosen by older people. A particularly corrosive emotional pressure, which applies to far too many older people, especially in our materialist, ageist culture, is loneliness. If we are a young person and we give ourselves a stroke, the pressures we feel generally have more to do with profound deprivation, performance insecurity and anger.

The important aspects to remember about strokes is that they deal with blood vessels (family), the brain (thinking) and (implied) affairs of the heart. Therefore, the most effective prevention and cure for a stroke is improving the quality of our Lives through healing our emotional wounds, deepening our love, honest communication and wise thinking, hopefully with a spiritual family of like-minded, like-hearted people.

RH+ AND RH- INCOMPATIBILITY

At times a mother's blood type will have a RH protein factor that differs from her child's. When their bloods mix during pregnancy or delivery, the RH- mother develops antibodies against her child's RH+ blood. During her next pregnancy, the mother's now-sensitized blood may mix with the new baby's blood and set off an allergic reaction inside the baby that can range from unpleasant to lethal.

The dynamics behind this rejection-through-the-blood is the mother's inner reluctance to have another baby (reject her family). She may feel afraid of the demands of eighteen years of responsibility and caring for another child or feel resentful about being out of social circulation because of child raising. The woman may also feel afraid of losing her non-pregnant body "status", particularly if she gets hefty ego strokes from her appearance.

That is what is happening from the mother's point of view. The child will create somatic problems from an allergic reaction to his mother's blood, which may range from anemia to jaundice, all the way to cerebral palsy. The child creates these conditions primarily as a framework for growth during his Lifetime and secondarily as a reaction to his mother's rejection. Thirdly, it can be chosen to symbolize a toxic element from a relationship(s) in previous lifetime(s).

CEREBRAL PALSY

Cerebral Palsy (CP) is a condition of brain damage which becomes apparent before the age of three. Cerebral Palsy can "result from" injury, infection from the mother, infection after birth or lack of oxygen from RH incompatibility. There are three types of cerebral palsy, each having to do with muscular disturbance; mental retardation may also result. CP is a very serious disease chosen for basically two reasons. One, to serve as a framework for growth in this Lifetime. In order to deal with a twisted body, many fine qualities of personal power, persistence and spiritual wisdom must be attained by the person in order to create a successful Life of self-love, personal power, self-reliance and happiness. This is especially challenging in our current performance, appearance-focused society.

The second motive I am aware of for choosing CP is to serve as a self-selected burden, designed to "redeem" ourselves from errors made in another Lifetime.

AIDS

AIDS, at the time of this writing, is a potential plague, cruel and devastating. It is not a punishment from Goddess-God (who would never punish !) nor is it a gay disease. AIDS is a syndrome in which our immune system is attacked and decimated by a very ugly virus. Without our immune system working well, we will likely perish.

We choose to acquire the HIV virus and thus place our immune system in jeopardy. We do this to indicate a huge emotional imbalance within us. The best explanation I have ever heard about AIDS has come from my dear friend, Lazaris. In his book, *Lazaris Interviews, Book I,*[7] he eloquently explains the metaphysical meanings of AIDS and the motives for its creation. Since AIDS is a world-wide syndrome, it has metaphysical meaning for all of us because we have placed it globally. I strongly encourage you to read Lazaris' full discussion about AIDS; it is very informative and inspiring. I will now paraphrase his main points about our motives for creating AIDS.

AIDS, like most other disease creations, is a physical metaphor signaling emotional imbalance. According to Lazaris, there are four motives for creating AIDS, four messages contained in this experience.

The first message is that the HIV-infected, disease-fighting-impaired person is likely feeling very defenseless. This is not just a feeling of situational weakness or vulnerability, but more of a Life-position of living as a victim. Far too many of us live feeling chronically powerless and knocked around. We are the ones who often lose, who feel we are at the whim of the outside world, who repeatedly get picked on. For many of us, this started in our childhoods. Understandably, we turned our victim experience into beliefs about Life and then incorporated this into how we saw ourselves. Then, continuing to attract more abusive experiences, we came to view ourselves as defenseless against a cold, cruel world where it is every person for himself against the others. We wound up feeling repeatedly weak, picked on, enraged, sad, powerless, empty, lonely and hopeless. This led to a most unfortunate, but understandable, emotional bottom line: self-pity.

The second message contained in AIDS is the polar opposite to the first; defensiveness. As just mentioned, many of us have been traumatized while we were vulnerable and defenseless as kids. As we grew into adolescence and gathered some semblance of power, we vowed we would never, never, ever go back into that weak, pick-on-me place again. So we often went totally the other way, built up our body armor, and became defensive, most often overly so. We banished the beautiful sensitivity of our Child Within to Emotional Siberia and then took on the world in a cold, falsely-protected, defensive way. We mistakenly sought refuge in denial and cynicism, a choice doomed to spiritual failure.

Many of us like to play martyr. We feel major burdens; are often greatly misunderstood and severely unappreciated. Martyrs abhor responsibility and seek to deflect it every chance we get. We are tired of being told we need to change; we want the world to change. We usually suffer well, and a lot, in silence. We sigh often, will not express our feelings or assert our preferences or inform others of their errors ("They should know!"). Then we blame them for not considering our feelings. Martyrs have frequent outbursts of anger, especially when confronted about our manipulations. We either requisition or imagine that they are persecuting us; then we use their "cruel" treatment to justify our own cruelty as we gleefully punish others and the world. We also can get incredibly pompous and self-centered: "My feelings.....my feelings...my feelings!" A true martyr hallmark: we punish a lot, especially those close to us. "That's just the way I am", we rationalize; "Since I am suffering, you can suffer, too (and I will help you)." Certainly, when we are in this defensive, attacking position, we are not giving, unless we do it to again feel overextended to promote more suffering (sigh). Yes, ok, we will give another time (sigh). Our martyrish Negative Ego is pathetically arrogant; we know everything and will not be told anything and cannot have anything suggested to us. Many emotional adolescents, who may be chronological adults, are immersed in this martyrish defensiveness.

Some of our common replies are: "Yes, I know that (but I won't change)", "I worked on that (so drop it)", "That was years ago (so do not call me on it now)", and " Ok, I'll think about it (hopefully you will forget to bring it up again)". Martyrish defensiveness is denial, a particularly lethal act because of our lack of responsibility and emotional dishonesty. Our Negative Ego encourages the lethal game of defensiveness because we wind up denying our heart. Walling off responsibility and love, of course, we will tend to fail, sinking into the slime-pit of lies and self-pity. Our Negative Ego is just like a virus in our consciousness: ugly to beauty and deadly to love and gratitude. Far too many of us tolerate it for too often and all of us pay the price.

The third message contained in HIV-AIDS is a loud signal that we are clinging to our past. We are clinging to what Lazaris calls a "blood anger", which is anger at our family members for emotional hurts they inflicted. Still unhealed, we are blaming them for setting up our unhappiness ("See what you did to me? I have a painful Life! See how miserable you made me? You are killing me! It's all your fault!").

It may offend some of us to think we would have, let alone act out such antagonistic attitudes in our health; but, yes, oh yes, we do. We also act out such attitudes in our relationships, work, money, automobiles and struggle in daily events. Holding ourselves back to point the finger of blame at "them" is never a smart choice, but, unfortunately, a common one. As discussed in Chapter Three, we sometimes retroflectively harm ourselves as a ridiculous way to get back at "them".

The final message contained in AIDS relates to a burning question many of us have hidden deep inside our minds and hearts. Because the true self has such an intense investment in love and because so many of us have been denied love so much, in many of us intensely burns the question: "Who loves me? Really?" Through our struggles with AIDS and its attendant conditions, we seek to satisfy this deep curiosity. It may seem strange at first blush, that we would disease ourselves to find out in a Hidden-Camera-sort-of-way, who really, really, truly, really loves us. We think something like: "Here I am sick; disoriented, disabled, unattractive, rejectable and weak. Who might possibly want me now? Choosing me now would mean they really wanted me." As our popularity count goes higher, some part of us feels better. Yes, there are indeed better ways to research this question (starting with ourselves). Most of us, however, are still very focused on the outside as our only source of love, strength and validation, so that is where we mostly turn; an unfortunate mistake.

The corrective measures to these AIDS messages, according to Lazaris, involve some very smart choices to continually make, even beyond healing our AIDS. The first corrective step to take is to be honest with ourselves and do an inventory of our participation with the aforementioned messages. The wiser us tries to tell us we are thinking/feeling defenseless, defensive, clinging to the past and seeking in unhealthy ways to find out who loves us. Thus, we would do well to heed our inner teacher talking to us through our body and honestly analyze our degree of participation with these messages, conscious or not.

The next activity for our healing is to know, truly know, the value we have as individuals. Each person is a piece of Goddess-God and is therefore good; our inner worth is always strong and as high as it can possibly be. From the separation of inner worth from outer worth comes the basis for valuing our selves; if we are good by Nature, then we are intrinsically valuable. And from our inborn value arises the basis for us accepting and loving ourselves.

The final action Lazaris recommends we take is to learn all we can about true success. To have the most fun, we need to learn what success really is, what success is to us individually and then learn how to change our self-image to allow for continually creating and receiving more success.

According to Lazaris, these are the prime treatments for the syndrome called AIDS. See how they pertain. Add to these emotional approaches nutrition, exercise, massage, psychodrama, radionics, homeopathy and allopathic remedies to create our own, personal healing regime. But start with our emotions. Easy to realize: many of us still have a lot to learn about love and the ways of love. The sooner we get about our true business of consciously expanding in love of self and gratitude, the better we will AID ourselves and each other into the higher realms of silliness, laughter and health. Whenceforth cometh unto us miracles, bounty, elves and all other kinds of powerful assistance.

Yes, we all can heal. Even of AIDS. Even at the last moment. Even at the very last moment. Use a vibration to change a vibration? Oh yes. Yes, as natural as using water to remove dirt.

AID ourselves. AID each other? Oh yes; as natural as using watery love to quench our spiritual thirst.

COLDS AND SINUS INFECTION

Contrary to the ridiculous advertisements in the media, there is no season for colds and sinus congestion. The advertisements are erroneously telling us that we are powerless, at the mercy of microbes and in need of their scientific, over-the-counter products. Not only does winter not cause colds, neither does sitting in a draft, getting our feet wet, kissing dogs or harboring airborne viruses. Many of us, however, give ourselves colds in connection with these events because of a mistaken belief that we are supposed to.

Colds, like every other event in our body, are a communication process. The usual symptoms of a runny nose, puffy eyes, sneezing, coughing and congestion in our chest or sinuses are the components of our body doing a slow motion psychodrama of us crying. Colds indicate sadness. If we give ourselves a cold, check to see if we felt sad two or three days before the cold's onset. I suggest then to highlight our sadness and feel it out; we can reduce our cold symptoms overnight. Sinus infections indicate more intense, more repressed sadness.

Another motive for giving ourselves a cold has to do with a desire to rest ("secondary gain"). Colds (and influenza) are common, culturally accepted excuses for staying extra time in bed, not going to work, taking it easy, integrating changes or getting extra attention.

In Chapter Five, our final chapter, we will discuss health, healing and our future as we blast our way into the evolutionary heritage that is this blessed and gloriously good time in history we call The New Age.

CHAPTER FIVE

HEALING AND THE NEW AGE

Many people will consider this to be the most exciting chapter of *BODY SYMBOLISM*. It is like the other chapters in that it is about the loving justice and honorable integrity of our Earth-school aquarium. This chapter, however, highlights the beautiful reality and feeling of *hope*, which is essential to all healing. Throughout this book we have implied and referred to hope for healing and relief from the miseries of disease and injury. In this chapter, we will clarify and apply that hope for healing in liveable, practical ways. This chapter can serve as a lens, through which the beams of other chapters' ideas are focused to inspire a higher resonance for healing. We will now discuss some powerful ways to promote healing and then touch a bit on what our future may look like as Paradigm Three, Metaphysics, becomes more widely accepted and integrated into our future culture.

HEALING

I define healing as the process of reversing the decision to live diseased or injured. That may not be a startling definition, but it is accurate. In Chapter One we discussed the Paradigm One and Paradigm Two views of what Earth Life is all about. We also discussed the paradigms' views of what disease and injury are and why some of us have them. Let us now consider these paradigms' views of healing.

According to Paradigm One, healing happens because God, the Chief External Authority, wants it to. Classic Paradigm One says we have a disease or injury because God wants to punish us, give us a heavy-duty test of faith or somehow purify us through suffering in our body (similar to the Hindu concept of Karma). So, if we start healing, Paradigm One declares it is because God felt we have endured enough punishment to "pay" for our sins, have passed our test of faith or have become purified enough in our Soul through the pitiful, pious purgings of our body. Healing, according to Paradigm One, is a welcome "all clear" signal from God. Paradigm One also says Humans cannot do anything great without the direct involvement of God; all healing must be handed down directly from God because Humans cannot do something that powerful on their own.

Classic Paradigm Two views healing as a series of corrective bio-chemical reactions. It claims that it is within the stupid, random nature of Life itself why some people are struck down with disease or injury and others are not. Those who get sick are those whose biochemical processes are not as strong as someone else's. These individuals are seen to be lacking sufficient genetic ingredients or else suffering from impaired molecular reactions, so that their "resistance factor" is low. Invading microbes, unfortunately, then grow easily in their Human host, much to his random "bad luck." Sadly for us, Paradigm Two says, this is how Natural Selection operates, thus weeding out and eliminating the weak members of the herd (Human = animal; society = herd). Obviously, the best cures for diseases are bigger and better chemicals which will strengthen our biochemical constitutions so we can better fight the all-mighty fight of survival that we have so forcefully waged against our "hostile" Earth environment for thousands of years.

Nagging concerns such as our mental and emotional states, according to Paradigm Two, are like so much dressing on a turkey - - nice, but not the real meat of the issue. Paradigm Two says healing results when the good chemicals beat out the bad chemicals.

HOLISTIC MEDICINE

Happily for us, there are some grand perceptual, PSYCHE changes occurring in some churches, research labs and support groups which will update our knowledge and help improve our relationships to our core selves, our health and our bodies.

In some big name and not so well known churches, for instance, a re-thinking is occurring through which a greater permission and experimentation is being achieved in healing. I have heard several anecdotes of healings and miracles happening because of an unwillingness to accept a disease. Thankfully, many churches and support groups have realized that Goddess-God is in *no way* interested in testing or punishing people. These groups of people have built their activities upon the concept that healings occur frequently. And they indeed do; all of us can experience one or several healings in our Lives.

There also have been several researchers who have been moving away from the classic scientific approach to healing and shifting to a more Humanistic approach (which, of course, includes science, but goes beyond and yet, rather poetically, winds up at the same place where science started; our mind. Interestingly, more scientists now seem to be searching through their calculations and intuitions for Goddess-God than those in religion; the religionists seem to have lost their curiosity and adventure, they seem to be stuck in dogma written hundreds or thousands of years ago). The expansive works of Hans Selye, Jose Silva, the Simontons, Gerald Jompolsky, Bernie Siegel, Deepak Chopra, Christiane Northrup and others have thankfully spurred many researchers, doctors and psychotherapists to become more holistic in their views and approaches to health and healing.

The holistic medical group holds the view that distressing emotions cause chemical and immune deficiencies which then lead to disease conditions. This is indeed accurate, and when this explanation is coupled with further understanding the metaphysical mechanisms of free will and Body Symbolism, our holistic group will really be on a roll into the future then! When our medical establishment comes to view each non-healthful body event as a *purposefully chosen construction* with definite emotional meanings, they will be in a very strong position to encourage true healing of a person on all levels; in belief, emotion, body, and spirituality.

METAPHYSICS AND HEALING

Paradigm Three, the Metaphysical view of Life, views healing as a person making a decision to live healthfully. Our healing process is one of our natural abilities, like digesting food, growing fingernails or creating a nose. In fact, in order to have a disease condition, we have to do a lot of inner work to get our cells to give up their natural inclination toward healthful functioning. We have to ask and ask and ask our cells to act hyperactive, inflamed, cancerous or whatever. Well, our cells love us a lot, so they agree to act sickly, but it is really not their first choice. But, for us? Hey, if we want a rash, we can have a rash. If we want a headache, we can have a headache. If we want gangrene, we can have gangrene.

Healing is the process of us deciding that we no longer want our cells to act out our previous illness request. Healing is us honestly, thoroughly giving our cells permission to once again function normally.

Please realize that healing is a thought, a vibration. The inner sounds of self-love, optimism and permission shimmer and glisten through our cells, creating and refreshing our body anew. Every Human is fully capable of generating a healing vibration. Medicine is in our head and heart. Let us be careful we not give our healing ability away, to those who work as doctors, technicians or to the drugs. We select our present and future experiences; start believing in ourselves - - take back our power. We can become our own best healer as we work with our medical consultants. Work to develop a positive attitude toward our healing treatments and ourselves. Honest, positive belief, coupled with a positive expectation, is the best medicine of all. Our belief, real desire and attitude is how we determine our treatment responses. The happy news is: medicine is in our head and heart.

If we consciously want to heal, but subconsciously do not want to yet, then we have a conflict, our energy is tied in a knot and we will probably choose to not yet heal (re: our discussion on recurrences in Chapter Four). But do not worry; these conflicts, though new to our awareness, are resolvable and we can be moving quickly toward our healing as we learn to authentically process and release them (especially if our inner work is aided by a competent, loving psychotherapist).

PRACTICAL SUGGESTIONS

Now, if we are ill or injured and decide to go for health, what happens? First of all, realize that our disease or injury conditions resulted from a free-will choice and that we chose them for specific reasons. Please refer to the list of basic motivations for creating disease or injury listed on pgs. 64-65.

If we unconsciously chose our disease or injury because of a desire for a framework for this Lifetime's growth, then please let us not disappoint ourselves too much if we do not let go of that framework for awhile, if ever. Let us not put ourselves down for it and do not let our family or friends come down on us, either. We or they do not have to like our condition, but if we want that framework, then it is our right to keep it.

For those of us who have not chosen our disease or injury condition to serve as an overall Lifetime framework, please realize that all bodily conditions are probable conditions and probabilities can be changed. I always encourage people to work on ourselves mentally and emotionally; however, this does *not* mean giving up regular, allopathic medical assistance. Medical intervention can be necessary and exceedingly helpful. Dedicated people who work as doctors, nurses and social workers, who believe in health and who are very kind, can assist us greatly. Just balance relying on them with meeting our main responsibility for our own healthful, creative thought. And please make sure we hold them accountable to the standards of competence and caring.

To those who have illness or injury or ever will have illness or injury, I suggest taking the following steps when working toward mental-emotional-physical healing:

STEP 1: *DETACH.* Detach your self from your current (temporary) conditions. We are not our conditions; they are separate from us. Detaching is the first step to acquire some perspective about what is happening to us. We are not a diabetic, an arthritic or a whatever. We are a spirit who has manifested a diabetic, arthritic or whatever condition in our holographic, physical body. Seeing our conditions attached to us, like barnacles on a ship's hull, can make healing much, much easier.

STEP 2: *TAKE RESPONSIBILITY* for our conditions, without blaming ourselves. It is ok for us to not like our conditions (indeed, necessary for healing), but definitely not ok for us to punish, blame or hurt ourselves because of our conditions.

STEP 3: *DRAIN* self-pity! Given what I wrote in Chapter Four about martyrhood, this next technique may seem paradoxical. This, however, is an absolutely profound, yet simple, process to keeping ourselves centered! Spend up to ten minutes at a time consciously feeling sorry for ourselves. Yes, consciously wallow in the self-pity we are most likely doing subconsciously! Let us not try to deny that we feel sorry for ourselves. Self-pity is how most of us comforted ourselves when we were kids! We did not know how to love ourselves, so we fell into pity. Most of us are still there, some just occasionally, but there. Why pretend this poison completely gone? No, that's a spiritual lie! Let us tackle it consciously and *drain* the *self-pity* out!

It sounds like this: "Poor me, _____ happened." or "Poor me, _____ did not happen." Follow this up by giving ourselves *credits* for all of our positive qualities and acts. Follow that up by consciously generating *gratitude* for the pieces of beauty already in our Lives. Drain self-pity, credits and gratitudes **(DSP, C & G)** equals one cycle. The more difficult our day is, the more cycles of **DSP, C & G** to give ourselves. The benefit of this is to release the toxic, energy-inhibiting, Negative Ego trap of the self-pity lie and replace it with the energizing, healing truth of our beauty, love and gratitude.

STEP 4: Realize what immense *POWER* we have, whereby we choose and arrange the events of our daily reality. Perhaps we have selected hurtful events at times, but that is just because of our hurtful beliefs, not because of a lack of worth or power on our parts. Please review dazzling Diagram on p. 56 to remind ourselves that our Life energy flows from the inside *out,* from the etheric into the density. Negativity in our beliefs and emotions become symbolized as the unpleasant events in our physical world. Our power is not in question, only our belief in our power! All we have to do is stop using our power against ourselves and learn how to focus our power in favor of ourselves (a relevant line from another book of mine: "Instead of pointing the garden hose up our nose, we could point it at the flowers."). Just because we have a disease or injury condition does not mean we are worthless, powerless or doomed! Understanding these truths makes it easier to believe in our power again, which is essential for receiving and healing.

STEP 5: Honestly *EVALUATE* why we gave ourselves our negative experiences. Please begin by reading the motives for disease or injury creation listed on pgs. 64-65. Which one(s) can we identify with? If our motive for a disease or injury creation is a Body Symbolic communication, then please ask the questions listed on p. 66. Using these guidelines, we can more quickly assess our motivations in creating our body problem(s). Thus, we can better do the psychological work necessary to change our thought-requisitions and heal faster.

STEP 6: *ASSESS* any limiting beliefs we have held or payoffs we have sought, with which we attracted the negative condition. Write them out. Beliefs such as: "If I want love, I must be passive;" "I must please everyone before I take care of myself;" "Mom/Dad didn't love me, so I must be no good;" "Good people do not show anger;" "Love is not meant for me;" "Success is not meant for me;" "God hates me;" "Life is harsh and uncaring;" "God only likes me if I act in a certain way;" "Punishing myself will make me better;" or "If I have it difficult, they will know who much I love them because I persist in the face of it all," etc.

Also, please let us research any emotional payoffs we may seek through our disease or injury. The usual ones are: manipulation, avoiding responsibility, getting attention, having an excuse for self-pity, giving into fear, guilt, self-punishment, proving ourselves or someone else right or wrong, trying to prove Life is hard, trying to punish others, hiding from abuse, hiding from personal power and creativity, belonging to a group or even trying to get some much needed rest.

Research and research and research again our conscious and unconscious beliefs and payoffs so we know what negativity we are working to remove. Be aggressive about it. Persist!. Again, the help of a loving therapist in discovering these hidden motives can accelerate our growth immensely.

STEP 7: Acknowledge, express and release any *ANGER* or disappointment with ourselves for attracting the negative conditions. This can be done well in a series of meditations or letters in which we really shout our anger at ourselves. Get it all out, With Harm To None.

STEP 8: Honestly **FORGIVE** ourselves for creating the problem conditions (more on this in the next section).

STEP 9: *AFFIRM* the rightness and power of our body. This may seem weird at first, but we may even thank our cells for acting dormant, inflamed or however they have been told to act. Please realize our body has not betrayed us and is probably quite capable of healthful functioning.

Most important to do: lasso the desired future into our current reality. Focus on a future time when we are well and carry that image with us. We can even think of a time in our past when we were healthy and use that as a template or pattern - - see and feel us being healthy back then and bring that health into our present and future!

In the here and now, keep believing in health. Meditatively tell our cells what to do now, give them new orders. Show them mental pictures of what the future healthy condition looks like. Keep investing in the healthy future and bring it into the present.

STEP 10: *SEEK* out healthy, self-loving people and do not isolate ourselves.

STEP 11: *RESEARCH* the many healing approaches now available and design a healing regime that suits us to a "T", one that speaks to the uniqueness of our Child Within.

Some may want to follow what our allopathic doctor says to the letter. Others of us may want to combine allopathy with homeopathy, with psychotherapy, with movement therapy, with Tai Chi, with humor therapy, with massage therapy, with nutrition, with psychodrama, with exercise, with color therapy, with herbal therapy, with sound therapy, with music, with family therapy, with crystals, with aroma therapy, with radionics or with whatever other healing approach we like. The important point is to know ourselves truly and deeply and then design and implement a path of healing that suits our Child Within, our spirit.

STEP 12: *MEDITATE.* Simply close our eyes, get as quiet as we can, count backwards from 14 to 1 and relax a little bit more with each descending number. Once we hit one, relax some more. As we do this, we lower our brain wave frequencies and have more mental energy available to direct in new, exciting ways, such as pumping up our desire for healing and our positive expectation. Also, we can channel more energy into our imagination to increase it and better, more emotionally visualize sequential body changes leading to our healing. As mentioned in Step 8, visualizing the future gives our cells a new set of orders and a new map for carrying them out more efficiently.

STEP 13: Find, *REBUILD* or deepen our relationship with our Child Within and our Adolescent Within. Research how to work with them to heal them. Help them, love them; *give* to them. Again, this is where a competent, caring, health-loving psychotherapist can be very helpful.

STEP 14: Find, *REJUVINATE* or deepen our spirituality. Our love of Life and love of Goddess-God are crucial to our reasons of why bothering to heal. In this regard, it is also incredibly important to clean up our act in how we treat ourselves and others. It is very wise and self-enhancing to stop any actions that even hint of cruelty or disrespect for emotion. So much better for us to become *givers* of love, kindness and inspiration, in every encounter we have (re: the discussion about speech in Chapter Three). On behalf of our spirituality and our evolution (our eventual future that we could make our present), we are required to eschew harmful vibes and become experts in generating uplifting vibes (yes, as difficult as this is, in every encounter we have). This is the absolute best gift to ourselves. It takes wisdom to know this truth and those who live it grant themselves a loving peace in their hearts that can, by itself, become a force that can transform any disease condition into its healed state. Our spirituality is about love; only love heals. Please grow our love. Do it now. Heal the wounds now; give love, freely. Please open up and become real. Only love heals.

STEP 15: A bit of repetition to highlight the importance: find our *FUTURE SELF* who is already loving and healed and meditatively ask him for inspiration and guidance in making the best choices we can. Send vibrational hooks to our Future Self and let him pull us there via inspiration. Keep feeling his healed-up state and infuse that energy and fun into our body.

STEP 16: Start *BELIEVING* in magic and miracles. They are the most real, you know.

FORGIVENESS

Forgiveness is an incredibly important experience. It is a force that can change and heal our Lives when applied well. Let us say a man has given himself a cancer condition in his right testicle. This indicates he is feeling much anger about lack of pleasure in his Life (second chakra) and about the burdens of the male role in our culture (reproductive system). So this man works to identify the beliefs he has internalized about maleness and find his angry feelings. After some or much digging, he may find that he feels angry at his mother and especially father (right testicle), as well as feeling angry with his wife, children and (our distorted) male society - - all for "placing" limitations and burdens on him (such as duty and obligation) and "denying" him his much desired fun. He then does himself the great favor of venting his angry feelings at these people and society, With Harm To None. Venting anger is well achieved through writing, pounding on pillows and/or screaming in the privacy of one's home or automobile; the anger does not have to be directly communicated to the people involved to relieve and heal ourselves. It just has to be released from our own emotional systems.

This is an important point to clarify a bit further. We do not have to directly tell the people who hurt us about our hurt and anger. In the case of our parents, they probably forgot about the events anyway and, for most of us, they probably did the best they could - - what they messed up on is probably what they were ripped off on.

When my clients and I got to this point in therapy, I find they fell into one of three groups. The first group worked to release their feelings and heal themselves in an emotionally honest, responsible fashion. The second group did not want to confront their true feelings about their "persecutors", especially their parents. I find many people, most understandably, want to make excuses for their parents' or siblings' or spouses' hurtful behavior. The last group of clients, conversely, wanted to tear into their parents or other persecutors and make their Lives as miserable now as the parents made theirs then. Though the last two approaches are understandable, neither is advisable. A balanced approach is the following:

1) Keeping in mind there is a difference between *intent* and *impact*, it is most likely our early caretakers and others had negative impacts on us and hurt our feelings at some time. If our hurt, sadness and anger are large (which we may reflect through our body), then it is our responsibility to remove those feelings from our emotional system.

Yes, most likely our parents or whomever made mistakes, likely out of their own deprivation, shame, disappointment and anger. Also, with Paradigms One and Two, we have all been living under a tremendous ignorance about the importance and beauty of our emotional natures; this ignorance ganged up on them and you and me and we all lost out. These factors are indeed understandable. They do not, however, take away or cancel out the feelings we created back then. If we have not yet honestly let go of our early feelings, they must be processed out sometime; why not now? I hope we will not make the mistake of using our parents' or whomever's ignorance or psychological problems to try to rationalize away our pain. We *cannot think away* our emotions! Face it: most of us were hurt. Understand why, sure, but please let us feel our feelings and release them, With Harm To None.

2) On the other side of the coin, our parents or whomever are entitled to make errors, even ones that hurt us. They, like us, have a right to be confused and distorted. Besides, we put them in our Lives for our own reasons. Sometimes our Child Within or Adolescent Within wants to strike out and hurt those who hurt us. Revenge is understandable, but definitely, *definitely* not ok to do physically. Our job is to heal ourselves, not perpetuate violent pollution with more low-level, hurtful behavior. Therefore, the Adult in us says NO to our Child or Adolescent and we choose to not act out our vengeful feelings. Instead we choose to release our anger and hurt on a pillow rather than on people. Hopefully, we also work to heal our Child and Adolescent through holding and nurturing them in meditation.

If we, however, want to communicate our feelings of hurt and anger to our oppressors, let us do it from our Adult so that we communicate without spreading more hurt around and lowering our true self-esteem. That way, we make it a spiritual win for us; because if it is not spiritual, there is no win.

Returning to the fellow with the cancer condition, at the completion of his truth-telling, venting process, he will have hopefully cleared out his emotional storehouse and will no longer have need for his bodily symbolic communication.

The next step in his (and our) healing process is to forgive those people and society for their errors. And the next step is to forgive himself for buying into those limitations taught to him. Forgiveness, you see, is true release. If this fellow does not forgive his oppressors, he will needlessly carry much anger within him. He will then turn his unprocessed anger sour in his guts or wherever and may communicate that mess to himself all over again (plus attract more outside oppressors!). This man does not have to forgive until he is ready, but to be whole and truly healed, he does have to use his spiritual strength to develop the virtue and skill of forgiveness so he can allow himself and others their right to screw up, let go of the past and live-love more fully now.

Those of us who will not forgive are likely stuck in the sickness of righteousness and vengeance; i.e. hurt Child, Adolescent and/or Negative Ego-arrogant-martyr. Or we could be those who receive payoffs for holding onto our hostility, such as a sense of phony self-importance, a sense of phony strength, a sense of (mis)direction in Life or even using our anger as an excuse to continue to punish, manipulate and live negatively. We usually reflect this sourness to ourselves through pain, disease, surgeries, struggle in daily events and even blocking our body's healing ability. Being unforgiving of others and ourselves is a resounding "NO!" to our cells natural desire to heal themselves. For some people, forgiveness is a difficult spiritual lesson which may take several Lifetimes to learn.

With this said, let us go a bit further. There currently seems to be quite a confusion about forgiveness; many people know that forgiveness speeds healing, so they slap it on this and slap it on that and expect everything to be ok. Unfortunately, many ministers and healers encourage this type of promiscuous forgiving: "I forgive everybody for everything they have ever done to me forever. And me, too. Amen."

Well, Humans do not seem to work quite that way. We need to process our feelings like we chew - - bit by bit (bite by bite). That is a big part of why we chose to be Human, so we could learn to deal with the truth of our minds and emotions. In other dimensions of spiritual development, the emotional complexity and intensity gets very, very heavy. Lazaris and Seth say beings there inter-penetrate and dissolve their emotions and personal boundaries in the emotions of the beings with whom they are communicating. Well, we could not handle *that much* togetherness yet, so we wisely came to Earth with its wonderfully clear-cut, physical boundaries to practice handling, bit by bit, emotional intensity, identity and blendings.

Therefore, it is important for truth's sake to *hate first* and *forgive later*. Forgiveness applied too soon can be used as another tool of emotional denial, which is just another rip-off. So, if we have a disease or injury which symbolizes anger, let us get into those feelings. Let 'em rip! Blow our jets! Please do not hurt anyone, though. Releasing hate by itself is fine, we do not need any ugly violence, thank you. But hate? Oh sure! My old phrase, "hate with gusto", is a good remedy as old as the hills. And forgiveness is a remedy which, when appropriately applied, allows us to transcend those hills.

OUR FUTURE

Because Humanity is just beginning to emerge from a blinding ignorance of our core, metaphysical essence, we have put ourselves through some gut-wrenching times in our history. *Billions of people have warped their hearts from lack of pleasure and betrayal of their insides.* It is so sad that many of us have been taught to think of ourselves as being unimportant and have treated others that way, too. Finally we are beginning to change.

We are in a wonderful time of history. We are living and creating an opportunity in which we will consciously decide whether our civilization grows healthfully or destroys itself. We are the ones who have chosen to be at the helm when our Earth-ship hits the challenging, narrow straits. Within the next fifteen years we are the decisive factor in shaping the next thousands of years.

An important note: whenever any new system of thought emerges, it often raises more questions than it answers. This happened when science was born. The early investigators were full of burning questions about the nature and mechanisms of geology, physics, botany, zoology, genetics, etc.

A similar surge of questions will likely be stimulated as we begin to understand metaphysics. Many of these questions will be about disease and healing (such as: Why are there geographic patterns of diseases? Why are there age ranges for some diseases? Why do women/men choose some diseases more than men/women?). Many queries will have no immediate answers and will require continued investigation. That there are no immediate, easy answers to questions that may arise is no condemnation of metaphysics, but simply a natural occurrence of the emergence of a new paradigm.

We now have an alternate set of ideas to explain Earth Life. It is leading to intense hope, freedom and brotherhood. Metaphysics is a story of Human worth-power, love and pleasure. We are finally coming to find out why events have been happening as they have been! We realize that Life is *not at all* hostile to Human health and happiness! Indeed, for the first time ever we see that, through interaction with The Great Principle Of Reflectivity, Humanity, like a tea bag in water, is totally immersed in justice.

The greatest gift Goddess-God gave us is the power and freedom of choice. We choose the course of our Lives. Our reality is *our* reality. It is a creation, a totally subjective, self-selected set of conditions inside *our* TCTCHB! It is a self-chosen sea of psychological symbols *we* surround ourselves in so that we may all the better reflect ourselves *to* ourselves and thus better find our true selves. Each moment we translate our Lives into this sentence: *Look what I am giving myself now!* Our wonderful, interactive environment is *passive* and we, the thought-emitting, spiritual ones, are powerfully, joyously active. There are no limits. Our happy interactive environment will go all the higher as we direct it to. So, just where will we steer ourselves?

THE NEW AGE

Before you read this book you probably heard others talk about The New Age and perhaps some of you have wondered what exactly that means. Well, as I understand it, The New Age is the first time this civilization gets to deal en masse with our true reality, which is our power to, moment to moment, choose our experience. The New Age is the first time we can decide en masse to be healthy, mentally and physically. The New Age is a time when we balance TECHNE with PSYCHE. The New Age is a time of self-completion, of emotional and spiritual Adulthood; a time a critical number of people choose to give up martyrhood. It is a time of a critical number of us choose to center our Lives around adult values of love, responsibility, honesty, consciously not hurting others, true power, integrity, compassion, self-esteem and service to others. Plus, have a bunch of fun!

We are moving into a time of history in which we will finally lift the oppressive weight of ignorance off our shoulders and hearts. We are waking up; waking up to a time in which many millions of people will finally realize the existence of The Great Principle Of Reflectivity and that we choose our daily events. That has never happened before. There have always been pockets of enlightened people, secret orders and yogis, with saffron robes and turban head-sets, but never a mass of varied, everyday people with awareness of metaphysical principles. This is the first time ever. It is difficult to say what will happen now or how it will unfold, but I venture to take a few guesses.

I think Earth Life is going to become a lot more unusual than it has been in the past. The key, the absolute key, to The New Age is that the structure of societal Life will change from objectivity to increasing *subjectivity*. Subjectivity is the basis of everything anyway, since we personally choose every detail into place inside our TCTCHB. Now we will enhance our relationship with our underlying subjectivity and bring it onto the surface of our Lives and societies, replacing the objectivity fiction (especially the ugly notion of randomness) we have been taught to believe and see for so long. This will likely be difficult for some of us to accept because many of us have sought to avoid the deeper, subjective aspects of ourselves and rely on the more shallow, objective parts of ourselves. We have been taught to avoid our emotions, Subconscious and Unconscious Minds, preferring instead to approach events logically and linearly.

The New Age is a time in which we will be invited to acknowledge, discover and harmonize with the subjective truths in the deepest parts of ourselves. We will need this knowledge before we choose to expand beyond the Earth aquarium. If we do not avail ourselves of it now, of course, we can have as many Lifetimes as we desire until we become ready. No rush to have fun - - whenever we want. The New Age, however, will be a welcome relief to millions of us who have hungered for deeper meanings, better approaches and increased blessings than The Old Age has allowed.

I think Earth Life will get quite a bit more exotic than it has been. Once some people get the hang of our self-creation ability, heck, we will do all kinds of funny things. Oh sure, we will probably learn to teleport ourselves around the globe, to be in two different places at once, change political outcomes with meditation, materialize money and whatever else pleases us. These events are available to us. Sure, even now. For instance, who right now is creating our nose? Who is giving us a little toe? Or something to read and a chair to sit in while we read it with eyes given to us by whom? By whom? Yes, we are that powerful. Moment to moment! So, if we want to levitate, we think it will help, go ahead, we are able to do so. We may have to learn how, or not, but we can do it. I think we all can. We may not want to and that is ok, too, as there are many other fine activities to invest our energy in; we get our choice. The absolute kicker about Earth Life is: we *always* get our choice.

As far as healing is concerned, why, we have not seen anything yet! Once we really get into our power and fully deal with what is possible, we could heal ourselves instantly, i.e. completely heal a broken bone during ten minutes of meditation. This is no exaggeration, as some people are doing it now. Just imagine how much better we will be at it with practice.

The current TECHNE push toward bionic limbs and organs is a nice option for some people and one that will not appeal too much to others. The balance here is to not rely on bionics to save us from ourselves. Other areas of scientific research have opened up possibilities for us to also consider. Genetics and *stem cell* research seem to hold great promise as tools to help alleviate some disastrous disease conditions. I am all in favor of pursuing these modalities of physical healing. We must be careful, however not to develop these or use them in unloving ways. Just because we can get an artificial heart or can replace nonfunctioning cells, does not mean it is ok to waste our time and avoid dealing with our growth issues of self-love and love of others.

I think those who dream of using bionics or genetics for "eternal youth" through a liver by Sony, skin by Monsanto or body by Fisher are barking up an ersatz, polychloride tree. If Humanity wanted to live forever in one Lifetime, we would have set it up that way. Instead we chose our system of many incarnations to give ourselves the most opportunities for spiritual growth. All of us have to go 'round and 'round with our emotional issues before we finally integrate those lessons into our mind. One Lifetime would be too stifling for the kind of growth we are after in this beloved, blessed Earth aquarium. Lazaris describes our Earth system as a speedy system, one in which we can learn and grow faster than in many other dimensions of activity. What might take us, say 90,000 years to learn here, would take millions of "years" to learn there. So, you and I and everyone else here chose Earth; we have a lot to learn and we are rather eager to do it - - multiple incarnations and all. Rather than rely on machines and TECHNE, it would be much better for growth purposes to put our energy into psychologically, spiritually healthful living in the here and now. Please remember (as mentioned in Chapter Two), when we die, an event that is scheduled *for us by us*, we will take our non-physical attributes with us, i.e. our degree of self-love, responsibility, honesty and capacity for loving others. Those blessed gems of consciousness are what indeed matter the most.

Once we get good at being fully Human and Humane, I bet we will not have much need for bionics or healing because we will not want to make ourselves so sick in the first place. As we better understand our Human nature, we will be more likely to move into love and then higher levels of love. And the more we love ourselves, the more we will love others, the more we will honestly, daily process our emotions, work for peace within and without and live more happily, with more abundance. So, if out of self-love we choose to be clear with ourselves, most of us will not have as much of a need for illness to get our attention and communicate our feelings. Let us be aware, however, that disease and injury are always ok experiences to choose - - some very spiritual people really do well with them. We would be wise to watch out for Negative Ego nonsense like: "Well, I never get sick, so I am obviously better than you."

Moving into increasing levels of love, we will generally be much more happy and healthy; and if we do give ourselves an illness or injury and want to get rid of it, we will understand it faster, process it out better and heal more completely than we do now.

So, Ladies and Gentlemen, I think there is a very solid basis for optimism and delight when we consider the future we could and likely will have. We are going to have to consciously choose it, though, and do whatever *work* is necessary to revamp our personal and societal belief systems to get there; a beautiful future is not going to be a cheap high. Our shared, mutual expansion will take effort, especially as we work to globally veto Negative Ego, bigotry, fear, guilt, violence, sexism, racism, graffiti and litter.

The purpose of this psychological work is so that we may create and enter into a space in which we may become loving and generous enough to treat ourselves as sweetly as we want to be treated. As symbolized so well in the body condition diabetes, when we martyrishly hold in our disappointment and anger or spew them on others, we turn our guts sour; the sweetness of Life cannot enter (though it really wants to). Our job in this New Age is to learn to treat ourselves so very lovingly that the very delicious sweetness of Life permeates our entire, blessed Being. Again, this can only be based on us knowing, deeply knowing, that we are truly good and deserving of beauty and bounty.

CONCLUSION

Please choose love. Please choose peace, non-violence and your spiritual self. Please keep in mind that Goddess-God loves us all totally and will help us with anything, to the degree that we stop our rejection of her and allow her entry into our hearts.

May you create your Life consciously and beautifully. May you bless your Soul, your TCTCHB, your body and your neighbors. May you mature well and vibrate peaceably in your true dignity.

Yes, find your light. And love your light, however much you currently know. So you may grow it into the true you and then you back into it. And then may you know the joy of blending your light with others and adding that light to the sum of all light that is this New Age, the beautiful light that is your Soul on the societal level!

WITH TEARS IN MY EYES AND HOPE

IN MY HEART, I SO MUCH WISH YOU

A WONDERFUL LIFE !!!

INDEX

REFERENCES

[1] The Denver Post, Friday, September 30, 1994

[2] Wilber, K. The Holographic Paradigm, Boulder and London, Shambhala Press, 1982

[3] Wilber, K. The Holographic Paradigm, Boulder and London, Shambhala Press, 1982

[4] Wilber, K. The Holographic Paradigm, Boulder and London, Shambhala Press, 1982

[5] Rybicki, R. *The Importance Of Being Human,* Royal Oak, MI, Arete' Press, 1980

[6] The Denver Post, October 4, 1994, P. 2-E

[7] Lazaris, Lazaris Interviews, Book I, Concept: Synergy Publishing, Beverly Hills, 1988